THE SIMPLE LIFE GUIDE TO FINANCIAL FREEDOM

Free Yourself from the Chains of Debt and Find Financial Peace

GARY COLLINS, MS

D0869955

THE
SIMPLE
LIFE

The Simple Life Series (Book 4)

The Simple Life Guide To Financial Freedom: Free Yourself from the Chains of Debt and Find Financial Peace

(First Edition)

Printed in the United States of America

Copyright ©2019

Published by Second Nature Publishing, Albuquerque, NM 87109

All rights reserved. No part of this work may be reproduced or transmitted in any form or by any electronic, mechanical, or other means, now known or hereafter invented, including xerography, photocopying, and recordings, or in any information storage and retrieval system without written permission of the publisher.

For information about special discounts for bulk purchasing, and/or direct inquiries about copyright, permission, reproduction and publishing inquiries, please contact Book Publishing Company at 888-260-8458.

DISCLAIMER OF WARRANTY

The intent of this material is to further educate you in the area of personal financial responsibility.

The text and other related materials are for informational purposes only. The data, the author's opinions, and information contained herein are based upon information from various published and unpublished sources that represent personal financial responsibility and practice summarized by the author and publisher. Even though the author has been as thorough as possible in his research, the publisher of this text makes no warranties, expressed or implied, regarding the currency, completeness, or scientific accuracy of this information, nor does the publisher warrant the fitness of the information for any particular purpose. Any claims or presentations regarding any specific products or brand names are strictly the responsibility of the product owners or manufacturers. This summary of information from unpublished sources, books, research journals, articles, and the author's opinions are not intended to replace the advice or recommendations of financial professionals.

Due to variability of how people manage their finances, neither the author nor Second Nature Publishing assumes responsibility for personal injury, property damage, or loss from actions inspired by information in this book. Always consult professionals first. When in doubt, ask for advice.

TABLE OF CONTENTS

GET YOUR FREE GOODIES

Get Your Free Goodies and Be a Part of My Special Community!

Building a solid relationship with my readers is incredibly important to me. It's one of the rewards of being a writer. From time to time, I send my newsletter (never spammy, I promise) to keep you up-to-date with special offers and information about anything new I may be doing. In my pursuit of a simpler life, I have moved away from social media. So if you want to be part of the "in crowd," my newsletter and blog are the place to be!

If that's not enough enticement, here's some spectacular stuff you'll get when you sign up for my newsletter!

- **Tabulating your monthly expenses worksheet.**
- **My simple savings technique I have been using for decades.**
- **The Five Simple Life Success Principles.**
- **Free chapter of "The Simple Life Guide to Decluttering Your Life."**
- **10% off your first order at The Simple Life website.**

You'll get these goodies when you sign up for my mailing list at:
http://www.thesimplelifenow.com/financialfreedom

OTHER BOOKS BY GARY COLLINS

The Simple Life Guide To Decluttering Your Life: The How-To Book of Doing More With Less and Focusing on the Things That Matter

The Simple Life Guide To RV Living: The Road to Freedom and the Mobile Lifestyle Revolution

The Simple Life Guide To Optimal Health: How to Get Healthy and Feel Better Than Ever

Living Off The Grid: What To Expect While Living the Life of Ultimate Freedom and Tranquility

Going Off The Grid: The How-To Book of Simple Living and Happiness

The Beginner's Guide To Living Off The Grid: The DIY Workbook for Living the Life You Want

PREFACE: WHAT IS THIS BOOK ABOUT?

FINANCIAL FREEDOM DEFINED

Today's bookshelves are collapsing from the tons of financial self-help books. These books promise to make you a millionaire if you'll just buy an overpriced course (from someone you've never heard of) or invest in a get rich scheme. Others promise to turn you into a master investor, making $50,000 a week, even if you have no experience and zero money to invest. These are just a few promises, and I'm sure you've seen your share of them.

Almost all these authors make outrageous claims about how they "made it." But a little digging reveals that they are in the same boat as most Americans – in debt up to their ears, barely getting by, probably full of fear and anxiety about the future. In many cases, the ONLY difference between you and them, is that they're trying to escape their financial problems by selling you a bunch of crap they have never used, and which they probably reprinted from some broke blogger or YouTube warrior.

Well, this is not that type of book! I make no guarantees of riches. But if you follow what I outline, I can say the probability of you having more financial freedom will greatly increase. Those of you who follow me and buy my products know that I never discuss or write about things unless I have first-hand experience with them. Matter of fact, I take great pride in that practice.

So, am I a financial expert? It depends on your definition of "expert." I will say after decades of managing my own finances, owning businesses and doing almost all of my own investing, that my knowledge is better than most financial "experts" around today. I also have a unique philosophy on how the everyday person can obtain financial freedom. This is because I don't just focus on finances. I focus on lifestyle choices.

How do the expectations of our society, including all its clichés about happiness and fulfillment influence your financial decisions?

How many experts in the mainstream financial services industry will ask you that question? And how important is this question to your total financial freedom? I won't candy coat it. We're going to discuss some things that will make you uncomfortable. That is the kicker. Positive change requires growth, and growth always involves discomfort and sometimes even pain. If you want the easy button, and prefer the soft spongy corners in life, this book is not for you.

So what does "financial freedom" really mean to you? Let's forget today's self-absorbed ambitions about being filthy rich and flying around in a private jet. I have a different take. To me, financial freedom is being able to live the life you want, without the typical worries, hassles, and constraints plaguing most people today.

To me, money simply equals FREEDOM! And the more money you have, the more potential for freedom you have; the more freedom you have, the less money it takes to maintain that freedom. If this sounds like a financial philosophy you can embrace, you'll be glad we found each other.

We'll dig into this deeper later in the book. For now, I want to invite you to start thinking about money in a totally different way than you have been taught. My guess is, as we explore this new philosophy, you'll slowly start to realize that you and I are a lot alike in our attitude about money, freedom, and life.

It is no secret that most American's are miserable; stuck in the daily meat grinder of a long (and getting longer) workweek and wearing themselves out on the hamster wheel of consumption. They are like cogs in the wheel of a brutal machine; a machine that literally runs off of the energy you and I invest into trying to achieve freedom and independence. I call this machine "**The Grid.**"

Most people in America are living as mere components of The Grid. Most of the work they invest into building up their own life is used to fuel this machine, and those who control it. But like any other machine, The Grid is governed by a basic set of rules. Those who understand these rules control the machinery of The Grid and benefit from the energy put forth by hard-working people like you and I. In other words, they leverage the rules of The Grid to prosper at OUR expense.

The ONLY way to escape this is to understand the rules of The Grid, and to turn them to our advantage. More on this later.

There flat out has to be a better way. One that makes sense. Now, I'm no bizzillionaire. I don't sail around in a "look at the size of my penis" yacht. I have no house in the Hamptons. Matter of fact, that lifestyle stresses me out. But, based on the interest people have shown in the simple way I live and how I'm doing it, I figure I must be doing something right.

Not to besmirch people who want to be filthy rich. But why should that be your primary goal? Having a "yacht-load" of money doesn't necessarily mean ultimate happiness. For me, it is about freedom and living the life you want to live. How much money does that take? It could be as simple as being debt free, or living a simpler life in a more laid back setting.

This book focuses on the assumptions about what will bring you happiness, and how those assumptions are actually making you broke. In fact, many of these assumptions are designed to leverage the rules of The Grid against us. Again, I'll explain what I mean later.

As our first step, we'll take a tour through the life of today's average citizen. I'll show you how every decision of your life, from childhood to adulthood, contributes to your financial success, or ruin. I think you'll be surprised to see how decisions and events, which seem irrelevant to your financial success actually make a world of difference.

By the time we're done, you'll have a clearer picture of how you became "Gridlocked" in the first place, and how you can start turning it around today.

1

MY STORY: HOW I FOUND FINANCIAL FREEDOM BY DECLUTTERING, MINIMIZING AND SIMPLIFYING MY LIFE

In the next couple chapters I will explain my journey to financial freedom and living a simpler, happier life. I have included this story in some of my previous books, because it outlines the valuable lessons I have learned. If you've read those books, you can skip ahead to chapter three.

HOW I ESCAPED THE GRID

As most of you who follow me or have read my books about simple living know, my journey didn't start on a whim. I constructed the foundation of my present lifestyle over a decade ago. It started with my desire to live more remotely and simply. Over time, it evolved into a complete lifestyle change.

First, I think it is important to understand that I grew up in a small town in the mountains of California. So my plan of living off the grid in the Pacific Northwest is not as drastic a stretch for me as you might think. I didn't start this adventure completely in the dark.

During my life, I have lived in many cities across the country. As I have aged, I have become more disenchanted with, and disengaged from that type of living. Urban living is not a bad lifestyle; it's just not for me anymore.

Having grown up poor in a single-wide trailer, with very few neighbors you would think I'd never want to return to such a lifestyle. That couldn't be further from the truth. Growing up that way gave me a different perspective on what matters. Sure, at times things were tough growing up. But it made me appreciate everything I had that much more. I now look back and consider myself incredibly lucky to have had these experiences. I was fortunate enough to know most of the people in my town. When I waved at them, they'd wave back. That's all but vanished from today's urban settings.

I have fond memories of racing home from football practice before sunset to catch an hour of bird hunting. Heck, I would have my shotgun behind the seat of my truck to save time. Yes, that would mean I had a shotgun on school grounds, and I wouldn't have been the only one. A lot of us were hunters. That's just how it was. Can you imagine what would happen to a kid doing that today?

Ok, I hate to have to do this, but I must clarify the above is not to represent my personal opinion, or political view on gun control. Yep, in today's nerf cornered, and easily offended society today, I have to put this paragraph and explanation in. If the above paragraph offends or drives you to leave a scathing review of this book based purely on this piece of my personal story, this book is probably not for you. Or maybe it is exactly what you need. Because everything I teach is about opening up your mind, and thinking for yourself without being influenced by such things as political tribalism. Matter of fact, I wrote and entire chapter about this in my book The Simple Life Guide To Decluttering Your Life.

The above is a part of my childhood and young adult story, and I refuse to remove it so as NOT to offend anyone, as some have recommended I do. Well, that's not going to happen, as I won't allow anyone to edit my life story in such a way. Ok, off the soapbox I go!

All this activity was based on pure simplicity. I didn't wear any special hunting outfit—just the clothes I'd worn to school. My shotgun was used and inexpensive. But it worked just as well as a shotgun ten times the price. In fact, I still own and use it today—40 years later.

At eighteen, I left for college. I had few opportunities to do the things I enjoyed growing up—hiking, fishing, hunting, or just being in nature. For many years, I yearned to return to that type of living. It is hard to explain to someone who didn't grow up experiencing this lifestyle. But I've always been the happiest when I had time to spend outdoors.

To me, life in highly-congested areas has become completely overwhelming. Why sit in traffic if you don't have to? The thought of going to the mall actually makes me cringe.

Now I can't state this enough: a lot of planning went into my escape from The Grid. I had numerous false starts, and mistakes along the way. But I wouldn't change a thing. Well, maybe I wish someone had already written these books! That would have made my life much easier.

Like most people today, I was locked into the day-to-day grind. I'd spent almost half my life working for the government in one form or another. Needless to say, I was completely burned out and questioning many aspects of my life. I remember sitting at my desk, after another joyous meeting with one of my bosses, thinking... **"What the heck am I doing with my life?"**

I was living in congested Southern California. I had a ridiculously expensive house—crammed with stuff I never used. I had more debt than I'd ever wanted or was even really necessary... I was slowly losing my mind. I knew I needed a plan. But what *was* that plan?

Although I know now that my dissatisfaction wasn't

unusual, I remember thinking... *"Is there something wrong with me?"*

If you feel this way, you are *not* alone. Since publishing these books, I have spoken to and received emails from hundreds and hundreds of people who feel the same way. More and more people are searching for a way to live a "simple life" of their own. They're no longer willing to accept the modern-day societal expectations, which force us to grind ourselves to oblivion chasing someone else's idea of happiness. There is a better way —a simpler, happier way.

HOW MY MISSION BEGAN...SORT OF

My original plan was simple; find someplace quiet to get away. I started looking at remote land or cabins in Oregon, Washington, Wyoming, and Montana. It was just a cursory look. Since it was the middle of the housing boom, remote properties were just as overpriced as the typical family dwelling in more populated areas. I called a couple Realtors just to get some information. But nothing serious came of it. At that point, I was a little discouraged that my plan seemed like a mere dream.

So I shelved my plan and continued with my daily grind. After more than a decade of research, I discovered that everyone goes through this type of discouragement. I've also learned that there's nothing wrong with people like you and me because we want to escape the soul-crushing machinery of The Grid. In fact, I consider this way of living more normal than the alternative. It's just less popular.

This is an important point. Especially if you've had people accuse you of being a "dreamer" or "luddite" for wanting a simpler life. I have never fit into the mold of today's American lifestyle: the nine to five jobs, the jaw-grinding commute, the cookie-cutter suburban homes. Like you, I have always been more of a free thinker. Sometimes, it just takes us a few failures to figure this out. Especially when we've spent so long living as a piece of the cultural machinery. I started my own side business a good ten years prior to hatching my idea of a mobile lifestyle as the means of getting out. I knew that in order to be free, I would have to run not only my own life, but possibly my own business. It is not always necessary to run your own business in order to live a more mobile lifestyle. But it sure helps.

The best advice I can give is if you're overwhelmed, or just worn out, with the daily grind, and if you're serious about living a simpler, more mobile lifestyle, you need a business model that fits that lifestyle. Today telecommuting is becoming more common for jobs, which don't require you to be in an office every day. So don't let your 9-5 job discourage you from planning your own escape mission.

MY REAL MISSION BEGAN WITH A KICK IN THE BUTT

Fast-forward a few years. My frustrations with the daily grind, and dreams of a simpler life were still in the back of my mind. But due to many life-changing circumstances, I wasn't pursuing my dream; I was still Gridlocked. The stress of trying to run my own business weighed on me. Numerous recent deaths of loved ones, including one of my best friends, hit me hard enough to knock my dreams out of my everyday thoughts. But I knew if I kept saying, "I will get to it next year," it would never happen.

So I rekindled my dream and put a plan into action. My thoughts about living a simpler, more remote lifestyle, had evolved a lot by then. I had started a new business. I had sold my house and most of my belongings. I was debt free and in a much better place to pursue my dream. My original plan was to have a remote getaway. But now, my plan was to live off the grid for at least part of the year, and to focus on being mobile rather than stuck in one place.

I was fortunate to have traveled all over the world while

working in the government. I also found the traveling to be addictive. I had caught the nomad bug and couldn't stay in one place for very long. The housing bubble had also taught me that the "American Dream" of home ownership—aka, saddling yourself with a big fat mortgage—is a chain around the ankle of anyone who wants a freedom-based lifestyle.

Most people assume a mobile lifestyle or living off The Grid means living in a beat-up van, cave, or shack with no running water, no electricity, and a cracked 5 gallon bucket for a toilet. Today that couldn't be further from the truth. You can now live a comfortable life on a piece of fairly isolated land. Or, you can travel around in a state-of-the-art RV. I know this for a fact! Not only have I been doing it for years, I have run into more people than I can count who are doing the same thing, or something like it.

While we're talking about false assumptions regarding the mobile lifestyle, let's tackle one of the biggest myths. Countless people have claimed that my story and my strategies for going off-grid don't apply to them because I am single and have no kids.

Further, they assume that a simpler type of lifestyle is unobtainable for "most people" because of this. The fact is, I have met so many people who are married with two to three kids, not to mention multiple pets, who are living *exactly* like I am.

In fact, I've noticed that people with kids sometimes use their family as an excuse not to pursue the dreams, which would make EVERYONE in their family happier in the long run. I'd also add that J.S. Bach had 20 children, and historians have said that his body of musical compositions was the most rigorous and expansive body of work ever produced by a single human mind. Obviously, having children didn't slow him down.

So I'm telling you with firsthand knowledge, *anyone can live this lifestyle successfully if they want to.* It all boils down to whether you want it and make it happen proactively or whether you just want to make excuses and complain about your life. People without kids have their own list of excuses about why they can't pursue their dreams. But excuses are excuses. Yes, that's a little tough love. But someone has to say it. This life is as simple as coming up with a plan and putting it into action, instead of waiting for a miracle.

I think the best part of this adventure is that most Americans can afford to do it exactly like I am. I do not come from a long list of millionaires. I do not have unlimited resources. Still, I won't deny, it does cost money. Especially in the beginning. I know there are books and seminars that claim you can take off with a hundred bucks in your pocket. Some people have even done it that way. But I like to live in reality and talk about what is plausible for *most* people--not a selective few.

Hopefully you will enjoy my adventure. Even if you're not interested in such a lifestyle. Maybe you will learn a little something to make your own life simpler and more enjoyable.

2

SO WHERE DO YOU START? YOU HAVE TOO MUCH CRAP!

Simplifying your life starts with decluttering your life. Decluttering your life starts with a solid plan, or set of action steps. As I preach in my other books—it is always better to have a plan and to take it slow in the beginning. Many people live cluttered, overly busy lives because of instant-gratification thinking. Ironically, that same thought process, often keeps them stuck. Meanwhile, great things come with time and perseverance.

As you now know, my mission to escape The Grid started several years ago when I decided to downsize. After owning several oversized homes, filled with crap I would never use, I decided it was time for a change. But that decision was just the first step. Even after acting on it, I was in the exact same situation. It took a LOT of time and effort before there was any external evidence that I'd made that decision.

The bottom line is, if you are truly interested in decluttering and simplifying, you are going to have to downsize. More than likely you will have to downsize big time! It will probably be scary, and even sad to "give up" so much stuff. But don't get Gridlocked by instant gratification. Don't be one of those people with a convoy of moving trucks lined up outside your house. Don't try to move immediately from the city to the country, rent multiple storage units to hide your clutter and pretend you got rid of it.

CONSUMER NATION: BUYING EVERYTHING IN SIGHT DOESN'T EQUAL HAPPINESS

Like most of you, I spent much of my "former" life being just what society expected me to be: the ultimate consumer and star member of The Cult of Clutter. It is no secret that most of us work hard to make our money, only to blow it on stuff we hope will make us happy. Now, I fully believe in the value of hard work. Working hard and earning an honest wage is honorable. But I do think we have our priorities out of whack today when we're working horrendous hours, often at jobs we don't like, just to surround ourselves with stuff that will never make us happy long-term.

Why do we buy the biggest house we can get and shackle ourselves to 30-year mortgages? Why do we buy cars we really can't afford? Why do we have closets full of clothes and shoes we rarely wear? Why do we stress ourselves out to have these things? Is it worth it?

Exactly! You can't answer that question because there is no logical or reasonable answer. But to me, the answer is simple. We do these things, and drive ourselves crazy in the process, because we've been told that this is how we find happiness. In today's society, having stuff equals having happiness. Trust me, I followed this mantra with gusto. I bought all kinds of junk I didn't need. So have many of us. So if this sounds familiar, you're not alone. In fact, you're probably more normal than you think.

If you take any young, sane kid and spend the next 20 to 30 years telling them they must do irrational things to make themselves happy, most likely, they'll do exactly that. Not because they're abnormal. But because normal people learn their habits and beliefs from their environment.

By the time those peer-enforced beliefs and behaviors become habits, the person doing them starts to feel like there's something wrong with *them* because they can't make themselves happy like "everyone else" can. So, how do you escape this socially reinforced cycle?

STEP #1: STOP BEING A CRAP COLLECTOR

Stuff is an addiction. Sure, it's more serious for some than for others. But like any addict, you must admit you have a problem. As a former "stuff addict," I like to use the term *junkaholic*. So, I'll go first to make this easier for you… *"Hi, my name is Gary and I'm a recovered Junkaholic."*

Now it's your turn. And believe me, you're going to feel relieved the moment you admit this. Why should we believe, and act as if, our primary goal in life is to compile as much useless stuff as we can? Why should we die among the heaps of our ingloriously obtained items? In the hopes that someone will find us before our precious "stuff" starts collecting dust, or one of our pets starts eating our faces?

As I said, the starting point is realizing that your life, freedom and happiness means more than your stuff. The idea that stuff will make you happy is one of the "rules" of The Grid. People who live by this rule become slaves to The Grid. People who leverage this rule by marketing stuff to the rest of us, well, they're the masters. Wouldn't you be more fulfilled by creating experiences, as opposed to acquiring more toys? Stuff-based happiness lasts a very short time. Once it's over, you need more, and bigger toys to recreate the feeling. The Gridmasters understand this, and use it to lock you into an endless cycle of consumption.

As you'll soon see, the secret to escaping the rules of The

Grid is to define and to live by your OWN set of bedrock principles. For me, I just had to realize that less was more. Of course, as is with my personal health philosophy, the interpretation of *less* will be different for each individual. But I'd relate it to the 2nd of my Five Key Principles, which we'll cover in the next chapter.

For example, my starting point was to greatly downsize my living space. I was paying a ridiculous mortgage for a 1,700-square-foot house in Southern California, and losing sleep over how to pay for it. I was single with two dogs. Why I thought I needed this much space is, even today, still a mystery to me. But if I'm honest with myself, I confess that I'd been brainwashed into thinking bigger was better.

Most of us borrow the absolute maximum we can afford, chaining ourselves to 30-year commitments (mortgages), not realizing that some round table of Jaguar-driving bankers in a $3,000 suits, decided that this was the best way to "own" a home. In the end, all it did was stress me out, financially and emotionally. I wasted a great deal of time on upkeep when I could have been using that time doing something I truly enjoyed. So again, if this sounds familiar, you're not alone.

That is one important point I want to make about our consumption-based lifestyle: not only does consumerism fail to make us happy, it actually takes time away from our true passions and our connections with those individuals we care about. And how can you be happy without those things? If that isn't true irony, I don't know what is. We spend a great deal of our lives pursuing things we think will make us happy. But in the end, they make us miserable and unfulfilled. Wow, the joke is on us, isn't it?

The great news is that we can change this. And I want to share with you my experience, and the steps to *happify* (my made-up word) and simplify your life!

STEP #2: EVALUATE YOUR CURRENT LIVING CONDITIONS

Okay, so now that we've both admitted to being recruited into the Cult of Clutter, how do you form your escape plan? Let's start by assessing your current living situation. Could you get by with less living space? I would say almost everyone in this country could answer *yes*!

For example, my first step was to analyze my monthly living expenses. This included my mortgage, insurance, utilities, and general upkeep expenses. It came out to an astounding $3,500 a month. For those of you who do not live in California, or one of the more expensive states, you are probably flabbergasted by that number. But let me tell you, that is *cheap* for a most people living in Southern California. Most people I know in California easily spend around $5,000 to $6,000 or more, for what I outlined above. I was no exception to this. But, now that I look back with my "what is important to me" clarity, I realize that this was absolutely nuts. The thing is we have been programmed to believe that spending this kind of money is not only ok, but is the norm—a belief which leads to a life of perpetual debt.

I still had about twenty-seven years left on my mortgage. So, I could look forward to spending a total of $1,134,000 (yes, that is over a million dollars) if I'd maintained that lifestyle for the remainder of my mortgage. Here is the kicker: Most of us don't maintain; we upgrade. So a million dollars is a low estimate. In fact, later on I'll show you some mind-boggling proof that, if nothing changes, you'll blow much more than that in your life.

We ALL have the capability of being millionaires if we adjust our lifestyle choices. That is a pretty astounding statement. Just thinking of the average person I know in California, their total would be easily close to double mine. Keep in mind that I'm NOT talking about your total living expenses. I'm talking about the *extra* money blown over a lifetime of consumption. Are you starting to see the insanity of our consumer-based economy? And consider this…

Did you know that if you're making a little over $30,000 a year you're in the top 1% of income earners in the world? According to the Global Rich List, a website that brings awareness to worldwide income disparities, an income of $32,400 a year will allow you to make the cut. Did you know that if you live in a place where the minimum wage is $15 an hour, you could make $31,200 a year just by working 40 hours every week? By the world's standards, the poorest people in the United States are considered some of the richest people on the planet!

Think I'm being dramatic? I assure you, once I got settled in my new, downsized place, I realized that the above is absolutely true. So will you. As I outlined, I was living in a three-bedroom home in the typical Southern California residential neighborhood. I had two and a half bathrooms, and a two-car garage. For a single guy, this is just way too much space. But, I also think it is too big for the average family, and I will explain why later.

But, it's important to understand that I didn't fully grasp how insanely excessive this was until I was out of the headspace, which comes with being an ultra-consumer. You'll realize the same thing when you make the shift for yourself. But until then, I wouldn't blame you for doubting these claims. While we're talking about downsizing your housing expenses, let's answer this common question…

IS RENTING AN OPTION?

As a transitional strategy? Yes. For example, if you're a homeowner planning to sell. Renting gives you a go-between while you downsize and get your plan together. That way, your plan isn't held hostage to the whim of the market. It also eliminates the need to make a big leap or an impulsive decision to buy a house to replace the one you're downsizing from. It's getting your toes wet, by wading into a simpler life, in a smaller dwelling, without committing to a 15 to 30 year mortgage. Obviously, you don't want to rent a place the same size as your current dwelling, nor even one that's bigger than you need. Rather, you simplify your space in order to force the release of clutter.

For example, you may need to get rid of the dogs-playing-poker print on the wall of your dusty man cave. You may have to part with 35 of your 50 pairs of shoes. That said, I do know people who have skipped renting, sold their houses and all their stuff and never looked back. Again this all comes down to your goals and lifestyle plans. We'll talk about how to pace and personalize your planning in the next chapter. But keep your mind open to renting as a transitional strategy. It worked well for me.

For example, after analyzing how much my house cost each month, I decided to consider renting. I realized I needed time to get my finances in order, work further on my business, and finalize my plan to simplify my life. House shopping is a big drain on your time and mental resources, so I decided to rent so I could focus on these other items. Plus I wanted to be mobile and not be tied down until I figured out my plan. The first place I checked out was on Craigslist.com. I will tell you, it was very discouraging in the beginning; renting in California is fairly expensive compared to the rest of the country. As I write this, another housing boom is overtaking California, and the prices are even higher than before. I guess some lessons are never learned!

When I was looking to rent, it was just after the housing bubble had burst (the start of the Great Recession), so everyone was trying to do what I was doing. So, the explosion of prospective renters was pushing rents even higher. On top of that, I had two large dogs; and most rental owners really don't like pets.

When they do accept them, they almost always hit you with a significant up-charge. If you're an animal lover, you know what I'm talking about. So believe me, I had plenty of obstacles.

This meant, instead of renting in my general location, I had to cast a wider net in order to expand my options. Having pets meant I had to include rural areas in my search; places where property owners are more understanding toward people with pets. I started by looking for two-bedroom places. I quickly realized that the price difference between renting and my current mortgage payment wasn't big enough to justify the move.

This forced me to start looking outside my (perceived) comfort zone. I started investigating studios, granny flats (i.e., small apartments attached to houses), and cottages (basically a studio house in which all living space is concentrated in one area, like studio apartment).

This forced me to open my mind to an entirely new life-style--one I had never experienced before. It simplified my idea of more than what was comfortable with at the time. Having less space forces you to have less stuff, which ultimately makes you happier. It was a pretty amazing mental shift at the time. I'll be honest I didn't foresee this possibility at the beginning of my search. But it turned out to be essential to the mental shift of simpler, happier living. So, don't get discouraged if you don't find the place you want right away. From my experience, making such a drastic change takes time because...

- You'll likely end up in dwelling types you have never experienced before.
- You will probably have to search in new areas that you are unfamiliar with, in order to find something that accommodates your current situation.

These two points are a really big deal when you're faced with them in reality. Change is always painful in the beginning. There is no getting around this. You have to realize you are making a major life change, and it *will* be uncomfortable. But all great things in life come with some scrapes and bruises. Remember that you're making more than a change in your living space. You're taking what society has told you, and turning it upside down. This is going to force a lot of rethinking about what makes you happy. You'll experience some self-doubt. You'll get criticism and puzzlement from those around you. The only way to avoid these things is to never make this change in the first place. The key is to stay the course, just keep going!

So, my search for a rental home in Southern California took about six months. I did a lot of research and soul-searching during this period, and ultimately, it paid off. I found a cottage with a full-size yard in rural San Diego. It ended up being the nicest place I had found, and it had the lowest rent, to the tune of several hundred dollars! Ironically, my landlords were the best I have ever had. My patience had paid off. The same will happen to you. You'll see.

Speaking of Landlords, it's important to evaluate them just like they are evaluating you. For most people, moving is not a pleasant experience. So my philosophy is to do it as seldom as you have to! When I moved into my San Diego rental, I knew I would be there for at least two years. I ended up being there over four years. That would have been a problem if I hadn't liked my Landlords. So it's important to evaluate them as part of the "package" of your new place.

Another thing to consider if how long you'll be in your new space before moving to the next step of your journey. Can you stay longer than planned if you need to? If you own a house, will you be able to sell it in a timely manner, are you upside down and willing to take a loss short term for long-term gain or will you have to try and turn your former home into a rental? I was unsure how long I would be in my new rental. But I made sure it was something I could do long- term if needed. Thankfully, I had thought that through because I ended up being in the cottage rental far longer than I'd planned, by the tune of a couple years. So, regardless of how long you *plan* to live in your new space, always ask yourself if you'll have the option of staying a little longer.

Now, I know most of you who are married and have children are going, "Yeah, that is no problem for a single guy, but our situation is different." This is true, but not as true as you might think. I know families who have reduced their living area by half with no problem at all. Sure, at first, they and their kids had to get used to the new lifestyle. But once they adapted, I never heard one complaint about the kids, or adults, not having enough space or privacy. Again, it is about facing the challenge and not giving in to the sentiment that it is "just too hard." If you have kids, keep in mind that single people have their own collection of reasons to avoid difficult life changes. But in the end, we all have to separate our excuses from our legitimate reasons.

Simplifying your life always comes with challenges. No matter how old you are, or how big your family is or how much money you make. But you have to keep your eye on the prize at the end. More financial stability and less stuff ultimately means more freedom, for everyone in your family. I'm not saying minimizing your living space and having more disposable income is the solution to *all* your life problems. But I can promise you this: it is easier to solve all your problems when you're not trapped by your living arrangements. Again, you'll see what I mean when you start your own journey.

THE PAYOFF

The Recession was not kind to most of us. For example, I ended up selling my house for a significant loss. But I had to make a critical choice. Either let my house possibly push me into bankruptcy, or deal with some short-term inconvenience for the sake of my long-term happiness. These were incredibly tough choices at the time. But I don't regret what I did for a second. Again, you'll realize this for yourself when you start making these choices.

For me, the payoff was undeniable. By forcing myself way out of my comfort zone, I found a great rental place for a great price. Now, I know you are asking, "So how big was the cottage?" My new rental place was around 475 square feet (based on my measurements). That's right, I went from 1,700 to 475 square feet, almost a 75 percent reduction in living space!

Do I recommend everyone make such a drastic change? Of course not. Again, it depends on your situation and comfort level. I will tell you that I have no regrets. Nor will I deny that the nostalgia for living in a big house again didn't haunt me from time to time. But I will tell you that the payoff made up for it, and then some. That's something to think about when you get overwhelmed by the changes. The payoff is worth it. So enjoy it and don't get stuck in your old thinking.

But, we should also talk about the tangible payoffs. How much money did I save? My $3,500 in monthly living expenses shrunk to $1,100 a month. And in addition to saving money, I was free of the stress of maintaining the large house, and yard, and everything in it. That payoff was priceless.

Another bonus was that I had to sell a lot of stuff because there was no way to fit it in my rental cottage. So, I made close to $10,000 selling all my extra crap on Craigslist,. I sold most of it in forty-eight hours! I can't explain the cleansing effect this had on my psyche and life. It was as if a lead weight had been lifted off my shoulders. This was my experience, and the experience of many of my readers. It will be the same for you.

By now, I hope you're realizing that all my advice is based on real-life experiences. If you've read my other books, you know that I never give you advice about things I have never done myself. So, believe me when I say that the payoff is worth it. You'll see.

For me, the bottom line was that modern home ownership costs more than money. It forces us into a situation where we can get stuck--sometimes for years, or decades. This is a huge drain on our time and energy. So, if you're busy and over-whelmed right now at the thought of following the steps in this book, don't worry. You'll be amazed at how much time you'll redeem by making these changes.

Case in point, I used my time in the rental place to plot out my next move (which turned out to be my mobile lifestyle and off-the-grid project). I made sure I wasn't rushing into anything I would later regret. Sure, we can't plan every detail of our journey and demand it to turn out exactly as we expect, but nothing good ever works out perfectly. But planning does make your odds of success much, much better.

OPERATION TRAVEL TRAILER: HELLO TINY LIVING

As I explained above, this renting period taught me how to downsize. But it also bought me time to get my ultimate plan together. By the time I had been renting for about three years, I had bought twenty acres for my off-the-grid house project. I was ready for the next step.

While building my off-grid house, to save money, I bought and lived in a RV, (if you are interested in starting that kind of journey check out my book *The Simple Life Guide To RV Living*. I have since learned that this is how most people build an off-the-grid house. This is important because off-the-grid homes aren't typically financed. And, it usually takes three to five years to complete the project. The payoff is you usually have little or no debt when it is done. The challenge is, you need someplace to live while the project is underway. For those interested in the off-the-grid lifestyle, I highly recommend you get my book *Going Off The Grid*.

Getting back to my story, I planned to live the mobile and off-the-grid lifestyle by starting with a travel trailer. That's where I ran into an unexpected problem…

A SNAG IN OPERATION TRAVEL TRAILER

By now, you know I don't sugarcoat things. So, I'll share a little flaw in my original mission plan here. I thought living on my property in my travel trailer was the perfect move. That is, until I built my house. Then my inexperience with travel trailers bit me in the butt. At this time I had a 4x4 V6 Toyota Tacoma, and my travel trailer was an 18' Ultra Lite. It was made to be towed by smaller vehicles. At first hearing, this sounds like a solid setup.

But my plan had a few flaws:

- My property had terrible roads—still does.
- The roads were very steep—still are.
- My truck at the time didn't have anywhere near the power to tow a trailer in the above conditions.
- Even if I could get the travel trailer to the property, I wasn't getting it back out.

Luckily I decided to do some exploring before I towed my trailer up. Sure, I realized my original plan wasn't going to work. But I didn't panic. Well, maybe a little. But I also looked for RV parks. There were more than enough in the area, and this ended up costing me only about $300 a month. I stayed at two different RV parks while building my house. To be honest it wasn't bad, and it actually made it easier to run my business, which at the time was teaching and consulting with clients on health, and a part-time college professor while my house was being built.

In the end, my oversight ended up being a blessing in disguise. During the time of towing my trailer around, I realized I really enjoyed that type of mobile lifestyle. To this day, I still own my travel trailer and spend close to half of the year living in and it traveling around. Had I been able to drive it onto my property right away, I might not have even ventured into that lifestyle.

That's a summary of my adventure and process building an off the grid house. As you can see, it required major decluttering and huge shifts in my thinking! During this process, I had to sell a lot of unnecessary items. I had to get my finances in order, while finding my path in life. There were a lot of other important details, and are essential to my current and continuous journey.

I hope this glimpse into my own journey will give you the courage to start your own soon. But it starts with getting your money in order. Most positive lifestyle changes require financial discipline. In fact, financial discipline is more important than financial prosperity. A point we'll explore in detail over the next few chapters.

SO, WHERE DO WE START?

In the following chapters I will be identifying the big elephants in the room. Starting with the Five Core Principles of Simple Living and how most people have habits, which contradict them and thus sabotage their chances of financial success. I know a lot of books on the topics of life simplification and decluttering do not cover these important pieces of the puzzle. I think you will be surprised by a few of them too.

Before we continue, let me clarify that you do not need to do things exactly as I have. This is your journey, and everyone goes about it their own way. I hope sharing my own story will help you gain some perspective to what life simplification and decluttering is all about. But, I also want to share what I believe are the bedrock principles of financial success, so let's get to it!

3

THE FIVE KEY PRINCIPLES FOR LIVING THE SIMPLE LIFE

So, how do you start on your OWN path to Living the Simple Life? Like anything else, you need a set of guiding principles. Otherwise, you're like a pilot flying without navigational instruments. You're forced to fly by your feelings, which any pilot will tell you is a direct path to a long, long dirt nap. Likewise, navigating your way to The Simple Life without these principles can end in crushing disappointment. That makes this the foundational Chapter of this book.

I came up with The Five Simple Life Success Principles almost a decade ago while helping people discover the path to optimal health. I consider these Five Principles to be the cornerstone of my philosophy. That's why you'll find them in EVERYTHING I DO. I didn't come up with these out of thin air, nor did I repackage them from other Self-Help books, as a lot of authors do.

The Simple Life Success Principles are the result of decades of trial and error. They're the result of my life experience AND my experience working with others. The Simple Life Principles will keep your priorities and deepest values in the FRONT of your mind while you're on your own journey.

As we're exploring these principles, please resist any impulse to assume that you've "heard them before." I realize they sound similar to things you've heard before. But as we unpack these ideas, I guarantee you'll feel like you're hearing them for the first time. I've found that when most self-help authors talk about one of these principles (though sometimes under a different name), they're just repeating things they've heard from other self-help "experts."

Imagine having someone tell you about another country, based only on things they've read in a book. This person may think they know what they're talking about. But they'd quickly realize how wrong they were after spending even a day in that other country. Likewise, I've found that most self-help authors aren't getting to the core of the principles they talk about. They're just filling your head with feel-good dogma that has no practical use in real life. Many of them do so, whether intending to or not, to make themselves like the Gridmasters we'll talk about in later chapters.

I've chosen simple names for these principles because it's appropriate for a book on Living a Simpler Life. These principles are so important to your journey that I recommend you print them out, and put them somewhere you will see them every day...

1. **Knowledge is power**
2. **Avoid extremes**
3. **Keep it simple**
4. **Something is better than nothing**
5. **Take action today and every day**

As we explore these principles, keep in mind that they deal more in the WHY than in how. We'll get into specific action steps later. Why have I taken the time to go over *why* to do things and not just *what* to do? Because positive and long term change is not about fads, quick fixes, or other self-help dogma. Quick, easy fixes are only useful for keeping you Gridlocked. This is why most people stay stuck there.

Principles point the way out because they cut to the heart of the matter. They cut to the "why," which always makes the how much, much more effective.

#1: KNOWLEDGE IS POWER

I have a simple philosophy when it comes to anything in life: *Knowledge is power.* Positive change is far simpler to accomplish and maintain when you're armed with correct, in-depth knowledge.

> *Dogma Alert: When I say "knowledge," it's important to note that I'm NOT talking about information. I'm not talking about a checklist from an "expert" in personal finance, health or some other subject. We're already swimming in that stuff. If information could make our life better, MUCH less people would be frustrated and unfulfilled. I'm talking about knowledge that's been tested and refined by hard-hitting life experiences.*

Too many people are trying to undo decades of bad decisions based on the same bad information that lead them down the wrong path in the first place. Almost every day, another article or news program promotes a means to living the "easy life," or "being happy, healthy and more prosperous." Yet, most of this information is just flat-out wrong, often dangerous, and sometimes a bit of both. Most importantly, I've found that people tend to cling to such information, and even defend it, without ever questioning how they came to believe in it. I'll show you some examples of such dogma when we talk about specific actions.

For now, I'm sure you've already suspected that a lot of self-help "knowledge" isn't very useful in real life situations. Instead, it's often shrouded in vague pseudo-science and cheesy advertising gimmicks. Other times, it comes from someone who is only speaking from their own experience, or with a rosy-eyed hindsight bias about what really got them where they are. They highlight all their smart decisions (which are often no more than dumb luck) and conveniently leave out all the bullshit they had to go through to make their life better.

Following such advice rarely gets you results in success. New habits are most effective when you know *why* you're developing them. Otherwise, you're likely to be swayed by the next fad or miracle product that comes along, because you never "owned" the knowledge in the first place.

That's why I started with this principle. This book isn't just about information. I'm sharing the knowledge I've gained from decades of trial and error, and from coaching others down this path. Most importantly, the other four principles will help YOU make this knowledge your own.

#2: AVOID EXTREMES

Have you noticed how people who read self-help books are chasing a new gimmick every year, or even every month? Ever wonder why they don't stick with one thing long enough to see results? Because most self-help philosophies deal in unsustainable extremes, and such actions defy the fundamental laws of life. For example, anytime I hear a phrase like "work just a couple of hours a week and make millions!" or "Insert product here, in order to cure your blues or feel good about yourself" I get really ticked off. Why? Because extreme claims may sound appealing, but they don't work in the long run.

Dogma Alert: There's popular saying that "moderation is the key to happiness." This is not what I mean by "Avoid Extremes." There are things in life that are dumb to even experiment with or to tolerate. There will also be times when making positive change requires you to get your ass in gear and do things that you believe are "extreme." But it's important to ask yourself whether you think they're extreme just because they're counter to the beliefs and the actions that have kept you stuck. What I'm talking about has more to do with finding your own natural "rhythm" to living The Simple Life.

Think about how the basic forces of nature, which have been working since who knows when, actually unfold. Night follows day, low tides follow high tides, seasons of scarcity follow seasons of plenty. Many animals that hunt, reproduce and thrive go into hiding or hibernation for weeks, or months afterward. Yet, the philosophy of The Grid tells us we can "skip" these natural rhythms and have everything we want, all the time, in exchange for minimal effort.

If the primordial powers of the natural world follow their own rhythm, why should we assume we can bypass this using some crap shortcut we read in a self-help book? Once again, it is just to get you to buy something you don't need, or to follow a BS philosophy that has no basis in reality. A slow, steady approach isn't as sexy. It doesn't appeal to our need for instant gratification. But a well thought out plan, followed day after day, week after week, will deliver positive *lasting* changes! Massive, extreme actions simply can't do that. Not if you want to avoid burnout and get results that last!

That said, I confess that, just like everyone else, I have fallen victim to numerous fads and promises of easy living. In fact, I'll tell you about one of my most vivid memories. I was young and trying to improve my health (a goal which makes you a prime target for hucksters). I remember waking up two or three times a night with a friend to do hundreds of push-ups, sit-ups, pull-ups and other exercises. I remember eating thousands of additional calories my body could never process. It seemed like a good idea at the time. But you might guess what happened. It's the same thing that happens to everyone who follows the "no pain no gain" routines at the other end of the spectrum. You end up fat, exhausted, frustrated, and hungry for the next piece of self-help dogma. Endless stories could be told of fad diets that wreck your metabolism and leave you feeling like you're some freak of nature because "the proven system," didn't work for you.

But these experiences teach us an important lesson: Fads are fads for a reason. They have no grounding in natural principles. They have zero value for the continued pursuit of genuine happiness and accomplishment. The "Fadsters" who push these promises just want to sell you something, anything, that will keep you happy long enough to avoid returning the product for a refund. They don't care if their product or system works for the long term or not. And when the trick-of-the-month doesn't work, or stops working, guess who's ready to sell you the next miracle product?

Quick changes tend to be quick-change backs. Extreme measures tend to create extreme backlashes, and sometimes the backlash is hard to recover from. But when you follow a plan that respects your own personal rhythms, you enjoy the process more, and the results are much, much more likely to stick.

#3: KEEP IT SIMPLE

The simpler your strategy is, the more energy you can pour into executing it. Overly complex strategies, on the other hand, chew up a LOT of your mental energy just trying to keep up with all the details. Our culture overcomplicates the pursuit of a healthy happy life by overwhelming us with products, fads, and gimmicks.

Have you ever run into someone who has found their niche in life? I'm not talking about someone who is complacent and going nowhere. I'm talking about that person who is content, relaxed and just flat out enjoying themselves. Everything they do seems to work out effortlessly. And you often wonder why things don't work nearly as well for you. Most people think such people are spending all their waking hours reading blogs, measuring and weighing their food, working out like an Olympic athlete, using every technology based gizmo promising simplicity. But that couldn't be further from the truth.

More likely, this is someone who has found a simple, non-extreme system for managing their lives, and they just keep plugging away at it instead of chasing every new fad or trend that's dangled in front of them. Their approach to life is so simple, they get to pour the majority of their mental and physical energy into making it work. Not so with most of us. We burn up a tremendous amount of energy trying to find the perfect formulas.

Dogma Alert: Simple does not always equal easy. I bet if you and I sat down, we could list several simple things you can start doing today to dramatically change your life over the next year. Why aren't you already doing these things? Because they're hard. Which I get. In my experience, most of the extreme and overly complicated things we experiment with are merely an attempt to avoid a simple, but difficult sets of actions. In fact, the Gridmasters in the financial world often exploit this tendency by selling you complex financial products that put more money into their pockets at your expense. I'll explain in later chapters.

For now, it's important to know that the type of simplicity I'm talking about only works for people who have the guts and the motivation to apply it with steadiness and consistency and to avoid extremes.

The saying "less is more" isn't just a clever tagline. It's based on the fundamental law of energy conservation. Birds don't struggle to fly, fish don't struggle to swim, trees don't struggle to grow. I hope from reading my story in Chapter Two and by following your own path to the simpler life, you begin to see that this life is more about subtraction than addition. But don't assume the subtraction will be easy.

Believe me. I know what it's like to overthink everything and to make living your ideal life far more complicated than it needs to be. I have been there. But once you cut out all the noise and clutter, you'll be amazed at how much everything comes into focus, and how much time and energy (mental and physical) you'll have to pursue what really matters.

#4: SOMETHING IS BETTER THAN NOTHING

At first, overhauling your entire lifestyle can seem daunting. Especially if you have really let it get out of hand. But here's a thought that always bears repeating:

"Little changes and choices add up."

When it comes to doing nothing versus doing at least something, something is always the right choice. No matter how "small" and action seems. Small actions repeated over time become habits. And habits shape our lives. Think of it like dropping a dollar into a piggy bank every hour of the day for years and years . . . eventually you'd have a nice nest egg. More importantly, you'd develop the *habit* of saying money, and habits tend to snowball over time.

You can always do something! Instead of bemoaning your stressful and unfulfilling life, answer this question: What would it take to make a better choice in this situation, at this exact moment? Even if it's only an incrementally better option, that little bit counts! Here are a few questions you can start with right now...

- Do you struggle with money at the end of every month? Analyze your spending habits and figure out a way to save more. No matter how small the amount may be in the beginning. Even a dollar a day beats nothing.
- Hate your job? Take training courses that will allow you to start your own company or develop skills to find a job you will enjoy. Even 15 minutes a day beats nothing.
- Can't get to the gym? Do 10 minutes of push-ups, crunches and stretches in your living room. If that's too much, start with one push up a day and keep at it until you can do 10, then 20 etc. Even a few push-ups are better than none!
- Sit at a desk all day with an aching back? Make it a point to stand up and move around each hour. If that's too much, start smaller. Even two or three minutes two or three times a day is better than nothing!
- Exhausted and haven't seen your kids all day? Turn off the TV and catch up together on a brisk walk around the neighborhood (yes, they may complain, but try it anyway!). If they won't agree to a long walk at first, ask them to go outside and walk to the mailbox with you. Even that is better than nothing.

If you read this list, and are thinking "But, that's not enough," you may be right. But it's enough to start, and if you don't stop, these little actions will become habits. Those habits will take on a life of their own. After a few days, weeks, or months, you'll start looking for ways to save a little more money, do a little more career development, exercise a little longer etc.

Dogma Alert: *There's an important difference between patience and complacency, which many of us rarely think about. For example, it's one thing to start with one pushup a day and slowly work your way up to 10, then 20, then 30. It's an entirely different thing to do one pushup, then sit down to an eight hour Netflix and Nachos marathon and say "at least I did a push up...something is better than nothing!" This Principle is not meant to inoculate you with overconfidence or to excuse building your life up with one hand while tearing it down with the other. The key is to start with small actions, slowly increasing their frequency and intensity until you find the natural rhythm we talked about in Principle #2.*

But if you never start because you believe you have to take big actions, you'll stay stuck. So, even when circumstances aren't ideal, don't assume you have no control. You can always control something. No matter how small. Instead of feeling bad that you can't do *everything*, do something!

#5: TAKE ACTION TODAY AND EVERY DAY

This is the next logical step once you've started taking small actions. Look, America is full of people who *want* to live a better more fulfilling life, but in reality very few ever take action to accomplish this. The difference between the people who dream about it and those who reach their goals is continuous action. Of course, a lot of people have trouble sticking with commitments. But in most cases, it's because they haven't grasped the Four Principles we just covered.

Here's the simplest answer: Happy successful people take action, today and every day. Their lives are an answer to this question:

> *"What's it going to take to stay on track and make progress today?"*

Maybe that means getting up a bit earlier to get to the gym. Maybe it means selling that sports car you really can't afford and buying something more practical. Maybe it means writing that novel you've been talking about for the last ten years. On that point, think about this: 10 years is about 3,650 days. A good novel could be 36,500 words or less. Could you write 10 words a day? Just think if you wrote just a 100 words a day, you would have that novel done in a year!

Small choices add up to a lifestyle that leads to long-term success and happiness. Taking big, extreme actions and trying to get the most done in the least amount of time often leads to burnout. That's the real-world truth.

> *Dogma Alert: There's a difference between the repetition of daily activities and true progress. Unfortunately, it's easy to fool yourself into choosing one over the other. If your actions aren't getting you the results you want, in spite of being at them for a long time, it's smarter to sit down and rethink your approach instead of just plodding along because you need to check the boxes on your daily to-do list. Thankfully, the other chapters in this book will help you take actions that have already been proven to work.*

So, how can you take action today? Every day? This ties into Principle #4: Something is Better Than Nothing. Maybe you can't get everything done you set out to accomplish today, or this week or this year. But do something. Don't give up and say it is just too hard. Don't get paralyzed by procrastination because things aren't going exactly as you planned. Always ask yourself...

"If I can't do the ideal, what else can I do?" **And never start a sentence with** *"I can't"* **when trying to change your life for the positive, because that is an excuse for** *"I won't."* **Get in the habit of saying** *"I want to change (X) in my life, where do I start and how do I do it."*

I like to call the above "positive change imprinting" I know it sounds really simple, but trust me it works.

Many times, you'll find that the "ideal" is an extreme place to start anyway. Start with something doable, and allow yourself to find your own natural rhythm in your own time. What do you do if your car breaks down, and ruins your savings plan for the next couple months? You pick it back up when the repairs are paid for. Then, you put additional money away for unexpected car repairs in the future. Treat this extra savings as part of your repair expenses. Put a little more money away every week. Even ten dollars is better than nothing. Believe me, a day will come when you'll have to pay that money for repairs anyway, so you might as well be ready.

No time for a full workout today? How about taking the stairs instead of the elevator at every opportunity this week? Taking the stairs may be hard the first time. You may not feel like doing it. But a day will come when you'll be glad you ignored that feeling and took action.

Life gets hard. Making better choices is sometimes inconvenient. But you have to ask yourself what kind of future you really want. Want to live debt free or improve your health? The secret is to make the right choices, slowly and surely, today and every day. Today's choices matter. They're under your control. Over time, these choices set the pace for whatever rhythm you get into six months from now, years from now, decades from now. But it all starts with what you do today. This is just as true today as it will be any other day.

That's the hard truth. But the good news is, once these actions become habits, they'll become easier. And. taking consistent action is the secret to forming habits and finding your rhythm.

Now, are you starting to see how these 5 *Simple Life* Principles are based on the development of positive and consistent habits? As I have outlined, short-term fixes never work long-term. You must ingrain and practice positive habits to achieve positive outcomes… it is truly that simple. One thing I can guarantee is that if you do not follow these Five Principles, or if you confuse them with their dogmatic counterfeits, success will be very difficult, if not impossible.

But, if you make these a habitual way of thinking, and acting, YOU might be surprised at where you find yourself in another ten years.

4

IDENTIFYING THE PROBLEM - CHANGING THE WAY YOU LOOK AT MONEY

Before we dive in, I want to challenge you to rethink your beliefs about money and personal finances. Most people see money as a means of gaining power/influence, or for buying stuff. Politicians and big businesses see it as a means of achieving power or satisfying greed. The everyday consumer might see money as a means of filling the void of unhappiness with shiny objects. In this chapter, we will focus on what money should mean to people like you and me.

I will say this with the most emphasis as I possibly can – if you want to be financially free, you must change your attitude about money. This is essential for finding happiness and living the life you want to live. For me, money represents... FREE-DOM! I see every penny I earn and save as an investment in my freedom to do the things I want to do, and to live the life I want to live.

I want to challenge you to think about money in the same way. Even if only for the sake of applying the tools in this book and seeing for yourself whether they'll bring you the happiness you're after.

To start, let me share what the word *freedom* means to me:

"The ability to live the happiest, and most rewarding life I can, without causing harm or intruding on other people's ability to pursue their own freedom."

Pretty straight-forward right? I'm guessing this is a definition of freedom you're okay with exploring. It kind of runs along the path of "treat others as you wish to be treated." It's about getting everything you want out of life without doing anything that keeps someone else from getting what they want. I think we'll agree that this is VERY different than the competitive view of money most Americans have today. When you look at money this way, your perception of money and its pursuit automatically takes on an altruistic color.

The question is, how do you turn that philosophy into financial independence? We'll talk about that in a second. First, it's important to understand why this view of money is so powerful. Because I admit, at first, it sounds a little pie in the sky.

In today's world, money is the most complicated concept or thing we've created that can create happiness or inflict misery. When used incorrectly, it can be a double-edged sword. This is why it is critical that you understand and master the concept of money. This starts with understanding your own motives for wanting money. People often confuse the desire for, and the pursuit of money as a form of greed. I both agree and disagree with this thought process. As I have pointed out, money equals freedom. So you must treat it as a very precious item that needs care and attention. If your primary focus is earning more and more money, at the expense of your aspirations for freedom and happiness, that's a problem. Unfortunately in today's world, greed has overrun governments, companies, and even the average Jane and Joe.

Here's a way to look at money today as it relates to freedom. The more money you have, the more freedom you can have; the more freedom you have, the less money it takes to maintain that freedom. Let me explain…

Let's say you owe $100,000 in student loan debt. Add this on top of all your other expenses, and you'll need to earn more money than your expenses/debt to pay down your student loans. This stops you from going on vacations and from paying off other bills, etc. Every dollar you pay towards serving your student loan debt is one less dollar you have to invest in living the life you want to live.

Of course, you could move up in your career, make more money, and pay more towards the debt. After some years of hard work, you could pay off this debt. When this happens you instantly get access to more of your monthly income. This is as good as getting a sudden raise. So now, because you've eliminated the debt, you have more money to live your ideal lifestyle. This means more freedom to do the things you want to do. And the more monthly expenses you can eliminate the more *available* money you will have. When you look at it this way, getting rid of debt is just as good as getting a raise.

The problem is, most people are so saddled with debt and other meaningless expenses, they're literally too "poor" to live the life they want. Even if they're making a decent amount of money. So if you feel this way, believe me, you're not alone. In fact, let's look at some crucial facts that prove we have lost our way when it comes to how we manage our personal finances:

- Between 1995 and 2015, consumer debt has skyrocketed. From 2000 to 2017 it doubled to $3.7 trillion, which is in the neighborhood of $11,000 for every person in the United States.
- A GoBankingRates survey in 2016, conducted as three Google Consumer Surveys, each targeted one of three age groups: Millennials, Generation Xers, and Baby Boomers and Seniors and found one in three people had

$0 saved for retirement and 23% had less than $10,000 saved for retirement. That's 50% of Americans who have less than $10,000 saved for retirement!

- Another GoBankingRates survey in 2016, found that 69% of Americans have less than $1,000 in savings.
- As of late 2018 the United States Government is over $21 trillion dollars in debt--almost four times what it was in 2000. In case you're wondering how this affects you, think inflation, cost of living etc.
- According to a 2018 article in Forbes Magazine, Social Security is already paying out more than it takes in and is on pace to run out of money in 16 years.

The above statistics and facts absolutely scare me and they should scare you as well. And if you think this is fear mongering, just look around at the people you know. How many of them are chained to jobs they'd rather quit because of their pressing financial obligations? How many of them are just two or three paychecks away from financial disaster?

It's also worth mentioning that debt puts time against you. Every year you spend paying down debt is one year less towards saving for your future. You'll realize how important that statement is when we talk about compound interest vs. compounding consumption.

Obviously, we have a severe spending and savings problem in this country—starting from the top down. But don't worry. This information isn't meant to incite panic or make you curl up in the corner mumbling incoherently sucking on your thumb. I'm a firm believer in recognizing the problem and putting together a solid plan. But the first step of any clear and practical plan is to define the reality of your situation. Debt is killing us. The solution? Get free from debt, start saving money, and start pursuing freedom!

That said, let's get a crystal clear look at why most Americans, in spite of living in the world's richest country, aren't winning financially...

IDENTIFYING THE PROBLEM

If you are serious about finding financial freedom and simpler living, you need to seriously analyze your financial obligations. Also consider how you're going to become debt free. I say this because, if you can't manage your finances now, you won't be able to do it when living The Simple Life. Even if you get there, it'll be no more than a mini-vacation, because you'll be forced out of it by financial problems. This starts with discipline. Just like your health (more on this later), financial discipline is essential for finding happiness and being truly free.

The negative Ned's and Nelly's will fight tooth and nail against this idea. They'll insist that they don't have a problem. Just like any addict they'll make excuses like... *"I don't need to change. I'm not like the rest of Americans. I'm healthy physically and financially."*

The problem is, most of them are comparing themselves to a nation of people who are sick and broke. That's a bad standard. But statistics don't lie. If you're reading this book I would say with a high level of certainty that you are part of the population who needs to change their life and habits for the better. Comparing yourself to people who are worse off won't help you do that. You have to set a higher standard, and make that your aim.

This means you need to have an open mind about where you are, and what we're going to cover next. I know. It's not all your fault. You and I have both made bad financial decisions. Just like everyone else. We are taught almost from birth to spend, spend and spend! The tools we need to be financially independent are not taught in school, or even higher education-- which is ironic considering how expensive college is these days... Is this by design? I would say, to a large extent, yes it is. In fact, I have a saying when it comes to the health industry today… *"There is no money in healthy people!"*

The same is true for the financial industry. Think about it. What's the best way to make money in the health industry? To keep us unhealthy and on a never-ending treadmill, chasing something we will never obtain. The whole time spending money we could be spending on other things. Think about the most expensive medical procedures, they're all designed to diagnose or treat illnesses. Name one expensive procedure, which is designed to make a person (who isn't already sick) healthier.

The same holds true when it comes to being financially free. The finance, banking, and credit card industry thrive on debt— which I'd equate to a financial illness. So what is there business model? Just like the health industry, they keep you spending, and purchasing things you do not need and cannot afford.

Most of the things we are told we must do in order to be happy today, are keeping is in a lifetime struggle to pay off debt. Thirty-year mortgages, five to seven-year car loans, student loans, credit card debt. It's all designed to keep you in debt and paying interest so that banks can build bigger and bigger buildings on every other block in your city. I will address each one of these, and give you a rational and doable solution. But let this sink in for a moment… *"There is no money in healthy people, nor in financially independent people."*

Healthy, happy and financially free people are, apparently, not the ideal consumer. If they were, we'd see an entirely different line of commercials and advertisements coming from the financial industry and the health industry. This is not to make you think of yourself as a victim. Rather, to show you that the people who you've likely been respecting as "financial experts," aren't interested in you becoming truly free.

You may be asking yourself, why I'm spending so much time

focusing on personal/consumer debt, and not on investing and wealth building. Because I have found the best way to obtain financial freedom and success, is to get rid of debt, and live debt free.

Have you ever wondered why those financial institutions who have created these tricky loans, also provide investment services? I don't know about you, but that sounds like the fox guarding the hen house to me.

It's like when the person at the Drive-Thru asks if you'd like to "Super-Size" your value meal. Believe me, they're not doing that because they want you to be healthy. They're trying to add to their "total revenue per customer." Financial "service" providers want to add confusing investment products on top of their tricky loans for the same reason.

Another reason, we won't cover investing and wealth building is that there are a ton of books on that subject. Unfortunately most of them are full of bullshit. I know. I have read more than I can count. But even the good investing books are worthless if you're too busy servicing debt to invest money. So again, being debt free is the simpler and more effective solution. Once you have that problem solved, you can take the next step, on growing your wealth. No reason to put the cart before the horse, right?

5

NO MATH = NO MONEY!

This will be short and sweet, but very important. I have never met an individual who is financially independent who lacks basic math skills. I know, a lot of people won't want to hear that, which is why most financial books insist you don't have to be good at math. But this is not true. When it comes to being financially independent, you do not need to be a math wiz. But you do need basic math skills.

Think of math as the ruleset that governs The Grid. Those who understand and apply basic math to their financial life, or to their business and products, prosper at the expense of those who either don't, can't, or won't learn and apply basic math. Banks and financial institutions don't just have more money than us because they're lucky. Rather, they know how to use math to their benefit, and to our loss. This doesn't happen because we're dumb or even because we suck at math. It happens because most of us flat out ignore math, while these institutions are busy systematically using it to their advantage.

Think about the rules of a game like tennis, football, baseball, Monopoly, chess, checkers, or even simple card games like

Uno, GoFish. Have you ever played one of these games against a more experienced person and had them use the "rules" against you? Young kids are masters at this. They invite you to play a game with them. You don't know the game, but you agree to play. So, they explain the rules to you, then halfway through the game they start using the rules they *didn't* tell you about to beat you.

Those who understand the rules of the game have a better chance of winning the game. Meanwhile, those who can't, or won't, learn and apply the rules have to depend on luck. Think about the last time you played cards with someone who knew how to win. If you won at all, it was probably because of luck. You couldn't duplicate your success, because you didn't have a plan.

The same is true of most people in their financial life. This is exactly what happens with most people and their money. They lose because they either don't understand basic math, or because they completely ignore it and live by their habits. And we'll talk about these habits, and where they come from, a little later.

Math is the ruleset that governs the flow of money on The Grid. Sure, emotions and discipline also play a role. But people who don't understand and apply basic math, never win consistently. They may have a few good weeks, or months, but for every two steps forward, they take three steps backwards.

And where does all that lost money go? Take a drive through the downtown area of your city and check out the three biggest buildings. My guess is, at least two of them, possibly all three, represent either a government building, or a financial institution. The rest of them will represent some other business that has applied a simple set of psychological and mathematical strategies to separate people like us with our money. This happens because most of us have no such strategy for our financial life.

Sure, most people will never need *advanced* math skills. I learned this first hand as a Mechanical Engineer major in college. After my first year, I realized that working towards such an advanced degree wasn't possible for someone who was also working a full time job. Of course, unless you're a genius, which I am not. So, I changed my major from engineering to Criminal Justice, that may not have been the smartest move, but fortunately it worked out. I will go over this more later in the chapter covering college and student loan debt.

Since then, I have never, at any time, felt like I needed those *advanced* math skills. Still, I have used basic math skills - addition, subtraction, multiplication, division and understanding percentages, almost on a daily basis. This is especially true when it comes to managing my finances. In fact, I'd say that if a person tells you they "never need" these basic math skills, they're probably not financially independent as a result of not applying them.

Basic math skills are pretty much all you need to manage your finances and become financially independent. That is not to say that these are the only skills you need. Far from it. We'll discuss the other skills for achieving your financial goals later in this book. The one thing I will say, if these basic math skills I mentioned above make you breakout in a cold sweat, you are in trouble, and need to overcome your fear of basic math. Otherwise, you will always be a slave to the Gridmasters who understand and apply basic math.

Again, I cannot make it any plainer than this: to this day I have never met an individual who is financially independent who lacks basic math skills. The focus of this book is not to teach you math, as there are plenty of online courses and books for that. I will provide you with some basic formulas. These will be useful for determining debt, interest and financial growth and helping you become financially independent.

But, the bottom line is that if you want to become financially independent, you need basic math! Anyone who tells you differently is just trying to sell you something, and probably has a very specific and mathematical plan for doing so.

6

UNDERSTANDING BASIC CONSUMER DEBT AND FINANCIAL CONCEPTS IS CRITICAL

One thing that has surprised me over the years when reading personal financial books, as I have read several over my lifetime, is that only a couple of them mention how simple and compound interest work. I will go one step further and say that I have found most people have little or no understanding of how interest rates actually work. If they did, most Americans wouldn't be knee deep in debt.

This could only be because people either:

- Have no understanding of how interest rates affect their personal finances.
- Don't care to know how.

I lean more toward the first option. As I have previously said, I think this is by design. Financial "experts" don't want people to know about this, because it's easier to sell people complex financial products when those people don't understand basic financial concepts. Either way, this is a huge problem that needs to be addressed.

So before we talk about the differences between simple and compound interest I want to give you seven basic personal finance terms and their definitions. For some, this may seem to be common knowledge. But, again I have found this to not be true in most cases. I'll start by defining each term, than give some examples where needed:

#1 - Principal: this term can have several meanings, but we will be discussing this in the context of borrowing money. For these purposes, principal refers to the initial size of a loan; it can also mean the amount still owed on a loan.

> *Example of Principal: You buy a house, and take out a loan for $100,000. The principal on the loan is what you owe at that moment, which is $100,000. After ten years, you've paid $30,000 on the principal and therefore owe $70,000 on your loan, which makes the principal balance $70,000.*

#2 - Amortization: this is when you pay off a debt with regular payments made over time. Your fixed monthly payments cover both the principal and the interest on the loan, with the interest charges becoming smaller and smaller as you make your payments.

> *Example of Amortization: let's assume you have a five-year, $20,000 auto loan, at a 6% interest rate. Your monthly payment is $386.66. This means, $286.66 of your $386.66 payment will go to interest while only $100 goes towards your $20,000 principal. By the time you get to your final monthly payment, $384.73 goes to principal and only $1.92 goes to interest. Mortgage amortization works in a similar way, we will get to that later.*

#3 - Interest Rate: this determines how much of your payment is applied to the principal (amount of money borrowed). This means, your interest rate is the *cost of the debt* to you, and the rate of return (profit) for the lender.

> *Example of Interest Rate: let's say you borrow $10,000 at 6% interest. This makes your interest rate 6 cents for every dollar you've borrowed. So the interest on your $10,000 would be $600 as calculated by the formula ($10,000 X 6% (.06).*

#4 - APR (Annual Percentage Rate): this is the actual yearly cost of a loan over the lifetime of that loan. APR is expressed as a percentage and includes any fees or additional costs associated with your loan transaction(s). This is where lenders get you, as they like to focus only on your interest rate. By law they must disclose APR, but it is confusing in most loan documentations, and likely on purpose.

> *Example of APR: let's say you take out a $200,000 mortgage loan with a 6% interest rate. This would make your annual interest expense $12,000, and your monthly payments $1,000 as a result. But let's also assume that your home purchase requires $5,000 in closing costs, mortgage insurance and loan origination fees. In order to determine the APR of your mortgage, these fees are added to the original loan amount, making your total loan amount $205,000. The 6% interest rate is then used to calculate a new annual payment of $12,300. Divide that annual payment of $12,300 by your original loan amount of $200,000, and you have an APR of 6.15%.*

Always, always ask what the APR is, or better yet be debt free and not worry about it.

#5 - Variable Interest Rate: your variable interest rate is the interest rate on a loan, which fluctuates over time. Home loans based on a variable interest rates are called " Adjustable Rate Mortgages" or "ARMs" (ARM). I'm sure some of you remember these types of loans. They were really popular, and partially responsible for, the 2008 housing bubble. These were loans which started out with low payments, but which increased in payment size as the interest rate increased. Over time, the owner of the loan (the home buyer), could no longer afford the monthly payment, which had originally been manageable for them. This was used to lure people into buying houses they really couldn't afford, even though the low initial payments made them feel as if they could. Again if these people would have had a basic understanding of how interest rates work, they could have saved themselves from a lot of financial trouble.

Example of Variable Interest Rates: Most ARM mortgages are locked in at a lower interest rate for the first 3 to 5 years. Once this period is up, you either have to refinance to lock in that rate, or your ARM payments will now start to fluctuate based on numerous factors (aka, "fine print") in your loan agreement. I will tell you this, in almost all circumstances your monthly payment will go up, not down. And the increase is usually a significant amount.

#6 - Simple Interest: when discussing simple interest loans (or other types of debt), it's important to know that the first payments of your loan goes toward that month's interest (aka, the lender's profits). Once your lender gets their money, the remainder of your payment goes toward paying down the principal you've borrowed. This way, each month's interest is paid in full. I'm not going to candy coat this… the above is a very simple description. Calculating this type of loan is more complicated than you think. I will be giving you a very clear example of just how confusing this type of interest is in the section discussing car loans. For now, it's important to know that the FIRST part of your monthly payment goes to paying the person you've borrowed the money from, not towards paying down your loan.

> *Example of Simple Interest: go back to the, $20,000 at a 6% interest rate, which we mentioned above. Again, your monthly payment is $386.66. This means, $286.66 of your $386.66 payment will go to interest while only $100 goes towards your $20,000 principal. By the time you get to your final monthly payment, $384.73 goes to principal and only $1.92 goes to interest. This means that, not only does the first portion of your monthly payment goes toward interest, the first few years of loan payments go mostly to servicing the interest on your loan. This applies to any loan payment, including car notes, business loans, mortgages etc.*

#7 - **Compound Interest:** compound interest, usually called "compounding interest," is interest calculated on the initial principal, which includes all of the accumulated interest of previous periods of a deposit or loan. The easiest way to think of compound interest is to think of it as "interest on top of interest." This is great if you're investing your money. But, it's terrible when you're borrowing money in the form of debt. The rate at which compound interest builds depends on the *frequency* of compounding. So that, the longer the term of the loan, the more compounding periods it goes through, and the more compounding of interest will occur. Think of it like a snowball rolling downhill. The bigger it becomes, the faster it rolls and the more snow it picks up, until it reaches the bottom as a boulder of snow. Compounding interest is how most typical loans today are structured, and again, it's good if you're investing and bad if you're borrowing.

Example of Compound Interest: Mike is 18 years old. Mike gets $2,000 as a graduation present, and puts it into an investment, which gives him 5% returns every year. By the time he's 19, his $2,000 has grown to $2,100. Now, he's making 5% on $2,100. By the time he's 20, his $2,100 has grown by $205, making it $2,205. Now he's making 5% on $2,205, and by the time he's 21, his original $2,100 is earning 5% on $2,315.25. As you can see, as his money grows, due to interest, his rate of growth also grows. This can add up to a LOT of growth over 10 to 20 years. More on this later.

Is your head spinning yet? I know mine is just writing these terms and definitions. Is it any wonder why we're so confused by today's consumer debt products? And we've only scratched the surface. I could write an entire book about consumer debt definitions, products and how they work. But for now, this list will do.

So, with the basics covered, let's dive into the primary factors keeping us Gridlocked by debt and consumption.

7

WHY HEALTH = WEALTH

I t's no secret. We're getting sicker and in more debt at an alarming rate. What most people never realize is that these two are directly linked. You might be scratching your head right now thinking...

"What does my health have to do with my financial well-being?"

"What does it have to do with making my life simpler and happier?"

I will say with 100 percent confidence, that it has a great deal to do with both! I have been involved in the area of health and athletics for over four decades. I have come to the conclusion that our declining health and expanding waistlines are a big cause of our shrinking financial freedom. So, I will say this – financial freedom *starts* with your health. If you don't make health your number one priority in the pursuit of financial freedom and of simple living, everything else in this book will be far, far more difficult for you.

Here's why I consider poor health, the main reason people never achieve many of their goals in life...

POINT #1: WE ARE FAT AND GETTING FATTER, BUT WE DON'T KNOW IT!

According to the National Institute of Health (NIH), data from the National Health and Nutrition Examination Survey (NHANES), 2015–2016 showed:

The average American is heavier, unhappier, and in more debt than any time in modern history. Matter of fact, according to Centers for Disease Control data on body metric, the average weight, when compared to height of men and women today, is a mere few pounds away from being obese. Let that sink in for a second. Our average weight, as a nation, is just shy of being rated as obese. If this trend continues, the average American will be considered obese in the very near future.

According to the most recent CDC data, the average American man is 5-feet, 9-inches tall and weighs 198 pounds and the average woman is 5-feet, 4-inches and 171 pounds. That's compared with 189.1 pounds and 163.6, respectively, at the start of the century (year 2000).

To put this into perspective, a man of average height is considered overweight between 169 and 202 pounds and obese above 202 pounds. A woman of average height is considered overweight between 140 and 174, obese above 175 pounds.

The Obesity Society, a scientific research organization, has classified obesity as a worldwide, non-communicable chronic disease. *"Obesity meets all criteria for being a disease, and therefore, should be characterized as such."* said Cathy Kotz, the society's vice president and a professor at the University of Minnesota.

Personally I don't consider a decision-based lifestyle a disease. I see it as a choice, and so should you. Either way, there's no doubt about how bad the problem with obesity has become. What most people don't realize is the devastating impact this has on the REST of your life – especially your financial life. More on that in a moment.

In 2015–2016, age-adjusted mean body mass index (a

measure of body fat based on height and weight ratio) rose to 29.1 for men and 29.6 for women from 27.8 for men and 28.2 for women during 1999–2000. A normal BMI is between 18.5 and 24.9. A person is considered obese at 30 and above.

Here is the kicker and true irony. Most overweight people are impressively unaware of how unhealthy they really are. For example, a 2018 survey by NIH asked U.S. households what they considered their health status to be – almost 70 percent indicated their health to be excellent or very good. Huh!? Are we completely delusional? Statistically (and visually, just take a look around) our health is getting worse and worse. Yet, most of us still consider ourselves not only healthy, but in *excellent* health. Maybe the next question in the survey should have been if they believed in leprechauns or unicorns!

And when it comes to the relationship between health and wealth, there is a direct statistical correlation. And when it comes to that, people are in even bigger denial than they are about the status of their health in general. According to the Joseph Rountree Foundation - the less wealth you have the more likely you are to suffer from poor health; the more wealth you have the more likely you are to have good health.

As I have said, I have been working with clients in the area of health for decades. A great deal of the information in this section will reflect my personal experience when working with clients in the area of financial expenditures. But we'll focus mainly on how one's physical well-being impacts their health and financial well-being.

POINT #2: BEING UNHEALTHY IS FAR MORE EXPENSIVE THAN BEING HEALTHY

According to 2017 data from the Bureau of Labor Statistics, the average American family spends $3,365 a year eating out. But my experience tells me that these numbers are incorrect. I think this number is much higher. Maybe people are in just as much denial about how much money they spend eating out as they are about the status of their health. For example, here's what I have found while working with clients.

My personal research has shown that eating costs about $10-$15 a meal, depending on what the meal is breakfast, lunch or dinner. Think about the last time you bought a meal away from home. I'm sure you'll agree that it is very difficult to eat a dinner meal for under $15 per person in a decent restaurant. So let's use some of that good old-fashioned math to see how these eating out numbers work in real life.

Let's use a family of four, as that is roughly the average family size today according to the U.S. Census Bureau 2018 data. According to the most recent Bureau of Labor statistics, 50 percent of family households are two income households. Most of these families eat at least one meal a day out, usually lunch so we'll start with that.

You would probably agree that $10 per person is reasonable for eating lunch out. It may even be on the low side, but I like even numbers. This means a husband and wife will spend $20 total, per day, 5 days a week. So, doing the math:

$20 per meal, times 5 (days per week), times 52 (weeks per year), equals $5,200 a year eating lunch out. Let that number sink in for a moment.

Now, from my observations most people spend far more than this in a day. So let's add some basic food related expenses below as an example.

First, we love our caffeine, but not just your average cup of black coffee. We like to add lots of chemicals and sugar to our mixtures. And of course, we don't really like making our own coffee. So, on average mom and dad each spend $5 each day on their caffeine fix, and since their addiction usually doesn't only apply to work days, it looks like this:

$10 per fix ($5 per parent), times 7 (days per week), times 52 (weeks per year), equals $3,640 a year.

Add that to our lunch total, and you've got a nice total of $8,840.

But we're just getting started. Since we're talking about the average family of four, we need to factor in the two children. For lunch and snacks let's use $10 per child, per school day.

$20 per school day ($10 per child), times 5 (school days per week), times 52 (weeks per year), equals $5,200.

Now we're up to $14,040 a year.

But we're still not done. Let's say each family likes to eat out once a week for dinner, at a cost of $50 per meal for the entire family…

$50 per dinner, times 52 (weeks per year), equals $5,200.

Now we're up to $19,240 a year eating out.

And we went fairly conservative with the above numbers. But I will tell you I have worked with families who I found to be spending close to or more than $30,000 a year eating out. Yet, they couldn't seem to figure out why they were unhealthy and broke. True, these families were on the high end. But I did not find them to be highly unusual when compared to most people I worked with. And MOST of them had no idea how much they were spending. So, instead of assuming you're "not spending that much," sit down and do the math yourself. I think you'll be shocked at what you'll find.

Now, let's do a little more math and really take a look at how these numbers impact your long-term financial totals. We'll use a 13-year time-span, since children spend about that much time in school (from 5 years old to 18 years old). Remember, we're working with $20 a day ($10 per child), five days a week, so...

$20 per school day ($10 per child), times 5 (school days per week), times 52 (weeks per year), times 13 years, equals $67,600.

Now let's apply similar numbers to mom and dad. On average, the parents will work for 40-45 years during their lifetime. We'll use the low number of 40 years in this example...

Lunch during workweeks:

$20 per meal, times 5 (days per week), times 52 (weeks per year), times 40 years, equals $208,000 total for the parents' lunches alone.

Caffeine fix:

$10 per fix ($5 per parent), times 7 (days per week), times 52 (weeks per year), times 40 years, $104,000 for caffeine fixes.

Notice I was a little more generous with this one, as I reduced your caffeine fix from 7 days a week to 5 to make it run more in line with your workweek.

Family dinners once a week:

$50 per dinner, times 52 (weeks per year), times 40 years equals another $104,000.

Notice I was really generous with this total as I only used 40 years again keeping in line with years you will be working. But I kept the total at $50 per meal considering you would more than likely eat out at more expensive places as empty nesters.

So what is your total cost of eating out over this 40 year period?

$416,000

Now let's add our total lunch and snacks with two children as tabulated earlier (add $67,600).

Grand total $483,600

Nope. There are no misplaced decimal points. Even using conservative numbers, the average family will spend nearly a *half million dollars* eating out during their lifetime. This is combining today's statistics, and my personal observations. And let's be honest, most families eat dinner out more often than once a week.

Here is the point I want to drive home – these are *static* numbers. I didn't factor in inflation and rising food costs, not to mention that the difference between eating out, when compared to eating home prepared meals, continues to climb every year. This number could easily be more than $1,000,000 (1 million) for the average family. Just for eating out during their lifetime.

Trust me, when I started breaking out these numbers to my clients, their heads were spinning. They had no idea how much money they were spending on eating out.

Now, I know what you are thinking… *"But Gary we have to eat! These are just normal living expenses! And what does this have to do with our health? We eat healthy when we eat out!"*

These are common objections, which I get every time I break out these examples. Let's answer the first question first...

On average, it costs about one third as much money (33.33%) to prepare a home meal equivalent to the meal you eat out. When I first started working with clients on their eating habits, I had them keep track of the costs, as well as doing it myself. I can tell you these estimates are highly accurate.

So if we apply this above information to our realistic total of $1,000,000 spent by the average family over their lifetime ($1 million times 33.33%), we *still* come to roughly $666,000 wasted on eating out.

Scary number right? So that debunks the "eating out is an inevitable living expense" objection.

As for the link between eating out and your health. Anyone who thinks eating out in today's restaurants and fast food joints is healthy is dreaming! I believe with absolute certainty there is a direct correlation between the amount of highly processed food we eat (which is mostly what you get when eating out), and the continued demise of our physical health.

The irony is that our laziness and inability (or unwillingness) to cook our own healthy food is making us broke and causing a host of health problems along the way. I say this because most people use the excuse that they just "don't have time" to prepare their own meals. But in the end, it causes us a larger waistline, a smaller bank account, and a shorter lifespan

For those who are still using lack of time as an excuse, I will leave you with one more example.

I want you to go to your favorite drive through fast food, or order-on-the-go, food place. First log the amount of time it takes you to go from your house to the restaurant, and back home again. Then, document the cost of your meal (to include tip if there is any). Finally, add the cost of the gas.

Once you have these numbers, buy the exact same ingredients for a similar meal the next time you go grocery shopping.

Keep track of the time it takes to prepare the meal and the cost. Don't add the grocery shopping time, because you were going to do that anyway.

Which one takes longer and cost more?

I challenge you to REALLY do this and come up with an answer that allows you to keep using lack of time as an excuse.

I have never, never lost this challenge. The eating out meal always cost more (much more) and takes more time once you add up the time spent going to pick up the meal. The healthy home prepared meal is always cheaper, and more time efficient. In fact, even if you factor in your grocery shopping time, the time cost is still lower to eat at home. On average it takes me 30-40 minutes to buy all my groceries for the week. Most people spend that same amount of time going to get ONE meal eating out.

I know what you are thinking... *"But Gary I can now order that toxic health destroying food and have it delivered straight to my home, I've found a time efficient way to slowly kill myself."*

That is like heroin dealer coming straight to your house and shooting you up... that never ends well!

Now, imagine what these numbers would look like if we factored in the increase in healthcare costs. The lost productivity due to eating processed foods and being overweight. Believe me, the numbers would be absolutely staggering.

Are you starting to see why I preach and recommend working on your health as the *primary* means to a simpler and financially free lifestyle?

Now, don't mistake me as one of those "you should never eat out" loons. I do not say that in the least. But eating out should be a *treat*, not a part of your everyday lifestyle. Another thing I will leave you with, most people who change their diet and start eating healthy, have a very difficult time eating out in general.

This is simply because it makes them feel not so good afterwards. I know. I'm one of those people. If you follow this path, it will happen to you too.

I'm pretty sure you've never read this in another financial book. But I think you can see now how vital a healthy lifestyle is to your financial freedom. Think about it, we just outlined how you could be throwing away over a million dollars on this. Is it any surprise why so many people in today's society are fat, sick and broke?

Are you starting to see why Health = Wealth? I hope so. Because we've got another big, big myth to bust now...

8

EVEN 5 YEAR OLDS ARE TAUGHT TO SPEND LIKE DRUNKEN SAILORS

Remember all that talk in the beginning of this book, about being bombarded with ads? It's no wonder we end up indoctrinated into the "spend yourself silly until you die at a very young age mentality."

The average American child, between ages two and eleven, sees more than twenty-five thousand advertisements a year. Global advertising spending is over $500 billion a year!

If our educational system and government were truly interested in you managing money properly and becoming financially independent, they would teach you how to open a bank account and save money, right after teaching you to wipe your nose, butt and tie your shoes!

Instead, most of us get more financial "education" from the ads we see than we get from the people who are supposed to be preparing us to succeed in life. We're told that getting an education will help us make money. But we get very, very little training on how to manage that money properly once we have it.

HOW I LEARNED ABOUT MONEY AND SAVING

Before the age of 8 years old (after that it was Poorville), my family would have been considered solidly in the ranks of the middle class. My mom and dad owned their own business in the small town where I grew up. This was how America worked back then. Sure there were big companies and businesses, but for the most part small businesses dominated the economic landscape in the United States.

I consider myself fortunate to have had this experience. It taught me about hard work, the value of money and the concept of saving what you earn (a hard lesson learned when my parents lost it all). Before I even started school I knew all the denominations of U.S. currency along with basic addition and subtraction, both taught to me by my parents.

With the big business economy of today, I feel that most children are missing the experience I had growing up. The result? Most kids never learn the importance of money, as it relates to freedom and forging their own path.

GLORIOUS MEMORIES OF YOUTH - ADS, ADS AND MORE ADS!

An hour on the internet, exposes you to more information— than you realize. Most of this information is useless and even irrelevant to your original search. I use the term "information" loosely, as most of it is marketing and advertising. In many cases, these advertisements are merely advertisements for other advertisements.

It is no secret our youth are spending a great deal of their free time on technological devices, primarily their smartphone. This is the gold mine for advertisers, as marketing companies know that the younger you are the easier it is to influence you to buy their products. And again, many times the "product," is just more information, more ads, and an endless chain of "click here to discover..." leading you from one pointless advertisement to another.

Do you remember those slick cigarette ads not too long ago with cartoon characters, and cowboys? Oh boy, you have to love those companies dedicated to getting you addicted at a young age then slowly killing you with their product. But today's endless breadcrumb trails of "advertisements for other advertisements," kills your dreams by robbing you of your time and attention. Whether these advertisers realize it or not, they're training you to be a consumer of advertising messages.

Below is a comparison list (not comprehensive, but an example) of the sources of information I was exposed to as a kid, compared to what today's youth are exposed to....

Young and Bright-Eyed Gary Back in the Day

Here's what I remember being exposed to as a kid...

- Television (no cable, a whopping four channels)
- Radio (terrestrial only)
- Books, magazines, newspapers (print only)
- Oral communication
- Educational institutions (brick and mortar schools)

Some of the above could, and did, have advertising, but at a fraction of the rate we see today. Remember those old commercials? I do...

"Hey, Mikey! He likes it!"

I threw that in for nostalgic reasons. But forty years later, I still remember it. How many commercials do you remember from when you were a kid? That's the influence advertising has on our minds.

A Little Slower, and Crankier, Gary Today

Compare the list above to what we have today...

- Television (cable, internet-based, satellite, access to hundreds of channels)
- Radio (terrestrial, internet, satellite)
- Books, magazines, newspapers (internet, digital, print, audio)
- Oral communication (maybe, if you're lucky)
- Educational institutions (internet, digital, print, audio, video, brick and mortar)
- Internet (general)
- Websites
- Blogs
- Vlogs
- Social media (increasing all the time)
- Smart phone
- Desktop computer
- Laptop
- Notepad
- Smart watch
- Health tracker

Today's children and young adults are mercilessly advertised to on these platforms. And think of how many buildings, buses, cars, even educational institutions look as if they're sponsored by every Fortune 500 company in the country.

When it comes to our youth today, I think they have very little chance of escaping the "consume until you die" mantra. Mainly because of the non-stop advertising campaigns aimed at them and other reasons I cite in this book. But with the right information, I believe they can be taught to appreciate hard work and to save for the future they want.

Hey, wouldn't it be a good idea to give them a copy of this book as soon as possible? I think so. But I may be a little biased. Either way, here's a list of things you can do to help them.

10 STEPS TO TEACHING YOUR CHILDREN ABOUT MONEY AND SAVING

1. Teach basic math skills, addition and subtraction, as early as possible. Yes, that means being a proactive parent. Don't expect today's education system to do it for you!
2. Teach them what money is i.e., bill and coin denominations), and what it is and is NOT for (buying useless crap!).
3. Teach them the concept of money and freedom, as I explained earlier in this book.
4. Open a savings account for them as soon as possible. Heck I would recommend opening one as soon as they are born.
5. Give them responsibilities; remember those things called chores, as soon as possible. Explain how the completion of these responsibilities will earn them spending money. For example, I would get my chore money at the end of every week as a child. If I didn't do my assigned chores no money. Yep, imagine that you have to actually do something to get paid.
6. As a part of number 5 (above) tell them they must deposit at least 50% of their chore money into their savings account and that they cannot touch that money until they are 18 years old.
7. Get them into the workforce, or have them create their own business, at the earliest age possible. Things have changed, I started working in a restaurant at age 13, but I'm pretty sure that is frowned upon these days.

8. Again, require that, they must deposit at least 50% of what they earn from their job or business into their savings account.

9. If they want something, teach them that they have to *earn* it. Today it seems like parents have forgotten this important concept. Nothing is learned from handouts. This is a valuable lesson if your child is to become a financially independent adult.

10. If you own your own business, teach them the basics of how you operate it, and the services you provide.

SAVE FOR YOUR FUTURE BY APPLYING BASIC MATH

Here we are again – using basic math! I will break this step down into two pieces. Remember, these are just examples to give you an idea of the concepts above.

First, let's say you start paying your child a $10 weekly allowance for completing their chores (remember no handouts). Say you start paying them for chores at the age of 5 and deposit $100 in their savings account to get them started. You may even come up with something creative for them to earn that initial $100 deposit.

Let's assume they continue to get paid for their chores until 18 (that's 13 years of earnings from their chores) and if they save 50% of that, (which is $5 every week). Now let's say they earn 2% interest (compounded monthly) in their savings account. Yes, this is conservative. But I would rather be pleasantly surprised than sorely disappointed.

Given these details, your math would look like this:

$10 per week, times 52 (weeks per year), times .5 (for the 50 percent of your $5 deposited into savings), times 2% interest, equals $3,986.70.

So, by applying this simple savings technique above, your child would have $3,986.70 by the age of 18. Ok, I understand this is not groundbreaking. But it's not an insignificant amount of money for an 18 year old either.

Now, let's take it a step further. Say they start working at a job at 16, and hold it until they're 18. They earn $10 an hour and work 15 hours per week for the full two years. Let's apply the same savings technique above to their work income.

$10 per hour, times 15 (hours per week), times 52 (weeks per year), times two (years between 16 and 18), times .5 (for the 50% - deposited into savings), times 2% interest, equals $7,952.38.

So, in just two years of saving half of what they earn, they will have an additional $7,952.38.

So, the grand total, if they continued to do their chores at home while working from 16 to 18 years old, would be $11,939.08.

But wait! We forgot to add the combined interest with chore money for those two years. So, it would actually be even more. But I didn't want to get into the weeds with additional math, as this is to be an example of the advantages of saving money in our early years instead of spending it on stuff. Not to mention that I used a very conservative interest rate. If things go well, and they save more than the minimum 50 percent, the above $11,939.08 could be closer to $20,000.

Even so, think of the things you could do with even the near $12,000 at age 18:

- Buy a reliable car
- Pay for a year of college (ok not some of those crazy priced colleges today, but at the State or Junior college level, you will probably get two to three years of tuition)
- Start their own business
- Or just keep saving the money and don't touch it!

Wow, we are only a couple chapters in and you are starting to see how much money we are wasting or leaving on the table! That is, if you follow the "spend until you die" philosophy of today instead of saving money. The kicker is, we are only talking about the power of saving money. There are a whole host of life lessons that will be learned as a result of doing this, and the other things in this book. Now that is a win-win, for you and your child!

9

CREDIT CARDS OUR GATEWAY DRUG OF CHOICE – IF YOU CAN'T AFFORD IT DON'T BUY IT!

I t's probably the biggest myth when it comes to driving us into lifelong residence at Debtville:

"You need to get a credit card as soon as you can, so you can build your credit."

I should know this myth well. It was pounded into my head at a very young age. Especially in college when I was told that revolving debt was the road to outstanding credit. What a load of absolute bullshit!

The model of building a good credit score is based on complete and utter lies, and is designed to get us into debt as soon as possible. The way you build good credit and have a high credit score is to get into debt. Then you make your payments on time like a good little boy or girl. The truth is, when you have less lines of credit, or if you pay them off every month, your credit score will suffer, and the harder it will be for you to get a low interest loan… what the hell!

Lenders, who are among the most ruthless and deceptive financial Gridmasters, know that the best way to get you into the "consume until you die" model is to lure you into the debt "heroin house" as soon as possible. Banks and credit companies do this by using credit cards. They do this for the same reason drug dealers give out free samples of their "product" to prospective customers. They're not meeting a true and healthy human need. They're creating a dependency. This is why I consider credit cards to be the ground zero of our consumer nation model. For most consumers, it is their first experience of buying on credit. And it's just the beginning of a costly, and life-long habit.

The primary reason Bankers, car dealers, mortgage lenders are pushing so hard for you to "build your credit" early on is so you can evolve toward bigger models of debt accumulation. They're literally training you to consume their product, even though you probably can't afford it. That said, the purpose of this chapter is to create some REAL awareness about the philosophy of credit-based financial "independence."

WHAT IS A "FICO" SCORE AND WHAT DOES IT MEAN?

To demonstrate my above point, let's take a look at what a FICO score is and what it means.

Here's a definition from consumerfinance.com:

> "A credit score is a number that is used to predict how likely you are to pay back a loan on time. Credit scores are used by companies to make decisions, such as whether to offer you a mortgage or a credit card. They are also used to determine the interest rate you receive on a loan or credit card, and the credit limit."
>
> FICO stands for the Fair Isaac Corporation. FICO was a pioneer in developing a method for calculating credit scores based on information collected by credit reporting agencies. Today, other companies also have credit scoring formulas ("models"), but most

lenders still use FICO scores when deciding whether to offer you a loan or credit card, and in setting the rate and terms. Banks may also use FICO scores when approving checking and savings account applications and setting the terms of those accounts.

FICO scores range from 300-850. Usually a higher score makes it easier to qualify for a loan and may result in a better interest rate. Like all credit scores, FICO scores can change over time according to your credit behavior."

If you read this very closely, you'll realize that the FICO score is just set of rules which the Gridmasters use to judge how qualified you are to be a lifelong consumer of their primary product. That product is debt. They judge your debt consumption potential using a simple set of mathematical equations.

1. 35% of Your Debt Payment History.
2. 30% of Your Debt Levels.
3. 15% of Your Length of Debt.
4. 10% of Your New Debt.
5. 10% of The Type of Debt You Have.

Simply put, if you stop borrowing money, your FICO score will go down. The true irony is that the better your FICO score, the worse you are at managing money and accumulating true wealth (freedom).

This is how your FICO score is calculated. To put this into perspective, think about how prize pigs are evaluated at those nice family-friendly agricultural competitions. The farmer gets a pretty Blue Ribbon and everyone applauds as he trots his award-winning pig across the stage. But every metric, including the pig's weight, muscle density, fat content, is based on how many pounds of tasty bacon they can turn that pig into when they finally slaughter it.

Likewise, your FICO score is a carefully planned, strategic

formula for determining how many dollars of profit a Bank or Lender can squeeze out of you every month, and for how long. If your FICO score shows them that you're a "Prize Pig" of a consumer, they'll be happy to set you up with a lifetime of credit cards, mortgages and other debt products. In other words, the reason the financial Gridmasters bring home the bacon at a MUCH higher rate than you and I is because they're taking it out of our hides.

PAYING OFF YOUR CREDIT CARD DEBT THE RATIONAL WAY

Let's look at how credit card interest is tabulated. The interest rate that you see on your credit card statement is shown in annual terms or (APR). Then, your yearly interest rate is divided by 365 (days per year). Each day, your credit card company multiplies that daily figure by your end-of-day balance.

For example, if your card comes with an annual rate of 16%, your daily interest rate would be 0.044% (that's 16% per year divided by 365 days). If you had a balance of $500, you would incur $0.22 in daily interest, making your next day balance $500.22. So, every day in debt is another day that you're accumulating more debt. This is good for your lenders, because it means you owe them more money, PLUS the interest on that new balance.

This is why, when it comes to paying off your total personal debt I always recommend you start with your credit cards. First, they tend to have the highest interest rates. Second, getting that first bill completely paid off has a huge psychological effect. It gives you the confidence that you can tackle your debt. Without these "small victories," most of us take one look at all our debt, then scurry into the corner and suck our thumbs saying "It's too hard!"

If you have multiple credit cards, start with the one, which has the smallest balance. Do this even if that means you only make the minimum payment on the other cards. This also means you need to stop using credit cards completely—**RIGHT NOW**. It doesn't mean paying off the lowest balance while you're still charging those $5 lattes and cool shoes on other cards. This is why it's also a good idea to hold a "card cutting ceremony" to mark the start of your debt payoff adventure. You might even do a dance with your middle finger in the air telling "the man" you will control me no longer!

Once you've paid off your smallest card, tackle your next smallest one. Do this until all your credit cards are paid off, finishing with the highest balance card last. The only time I recommend you deviate from this is when one of your credit cards has an interest rate that's far higher than the others. But you should still pay off the smallest card first to get your feet wet and develop some discipline. If you have cards with 25% plus interest rates, move to them next.

If you have the discipline, and have a card that accumulates cash points and can pay it off every month, you might keep one card open. For example, I have a credit card that collects cash points and I use this extra money to transfer into a savings account. But here's the catch—I pay that credit card off completely every month before any interest can be accrued. So those cash points are like free money! I know very few people have this type of discipline. But if you can do it, I highly recommend it.

I'm also a realist. In my financial model, it's not a sin to have one credit card for emergencies. But an emergency is not a new dress or set of golf clubs. If you have mastered your financial discipline and can handle having an emergency credit card, I would advise you to lock it up in a safe place. Don't carry it in your wallet or purse.

Once you have your credit cards paid off, you'll be ahead of almost every American today. That should motivate you to look at your other expenses and pay those off as well. The best part is that you'll now have more free income to pay off any remaining debts (we'll talk about how to do this later).

CREDIT CARD MATH TIME!

Now that we know credit cards are the gateway drug to lifelong financial ruin, let's see how the numbers add up. We'll start with some alarming credit card stats:

- The average American in 2018 has a credit card balance of $4,293.
- The average American family in 2018 carries $10,400 in credit card debt.
- A recent WalletHub survey found that more than 1 in 3 people are afraid of maxing out their credit cards when making a purchase over $100.
- Americans as a country in 2018 exceeded for the first time $1 trillion in credit card debt.
- Americans paid $104 billion in credit card interest and fees for the twelve months leading up to August 2018. That's $823.96 in interest and fees for every household in the U.S. with a total of 126.6 million households.
- The average American can't afford a $400 emergency.
- Credit card interest is rising, now averaging 17.41 percent.

Again, let us say you get your first credit card at age 18, and have one until you pass away. Trust me that's how the banks want it. And since I like round numbers, let's say you live an additional 60 years past the age of 18.

60 years times $823.96 (interest per year based on the above numbers), equals $49,437.60... in INTEREST alone.

That doesn't include all the useless crap bought with those credit cards. Also, according to the above calculation, the average American can expect to pay almost $50,000 in credit card interest during their lifetime.

By the way, it might interest you to know that Banks and other credit pushers have a rather morbid term for the above number. It's called the "Lifetime Customer Value." That is, the total amount of "value," they can earn from turning you and I into life-long borrowers. And the "better" your FICO score, the more of a prize you are for those lenders. It tells them how much potential profit they can get out of you before you finally buy the farm.

Of course the above lifetime value was determined using static numbers. In reality it will probably be much higher when you factor in rising debt and spending. Are you starting to see why these companies are so aggressive in convincing you to start borrowing at as young an age as possible?

Here is the kicker…we are just getting started when it comes to the high price of being a debt consumer. The average American family spends over a half-million dollars eating out and ruining their health. Most of them are doing that using credit cards, WHILE buying tons of other things they literally cannot afford.

So before we continue, let this sink in…I just showed you that you will spend over $500,000 during your lifetime, and get absolutely nothing in return!

Are we having fun yet? Just wait, it gets much better. We haven't hit the big one; financing the supposed American dream… your house, which we will cover in a later chapter.

10

DRIVING ON THE HIGHWAY TO DEBT HELL

If there is one place I'll give you a little leeway in your pursuit of financial freedom, and I mean very little, it is in the area of automobile financing. There are two reasons for this; first for almost everyone, a reliable automobile is essential for earning the money to become financially independent. Secondly, car loans usually have the lowest interest rates and better terms than most things you'll finance during your lifetime. Of course, this depends on your credit rating. If you have bad credit or no credit rating this can drastically change the affordability of your car loan.

The problem is, most people impulse buy on cars that do not fit their life goals or their financial capabilities. Just like many things we purchase today, we consider our automobile a status symbol instead of tool for achieving our goals. I know this all too well. If I have one weakness in the area of money, it's that I love cars.

During my younger years, I was more worried about attracting the ladies with a cool car than I was about how this string of terrible financial decisions would affect me down the road. With that said, I finally recognized that my weakness wasn't going to be hookers or cocaine, but cars. So I needed to fix the problem. At the end of this chapter, I'll give you some examples of how I beat my car addiction without incurring additional financial burden.

First, let's take another look at some dreadful facts about car financing...

- About 44% of American adults are relying on an auto loan to pay for their car.
- The average monthly payment on a new car was $523 in the first quarter of 2018.
- In 2018 a record 7 million Americans were 90 days or more behind on their auto loan payments.
- In January 2018, Kelley Blue Book reported the estimated average transaction price (ATP) for light vehicles in the United States was $36,270.
- At the close of the fourth quarter of 2017, the average amount of new car financing in the U.S. was $31,099.
- In 2017, average car ownership costs of vehicles driven 15,000 miles a year were $8,469 a year, or about $706 a month.
- Cars lose around 20% to 30% of their value in the first year you own them. Over each of the next five years, they lose another 15% to 18%.

Over the last 10 years car prices have skyrocketed. We are quickly approaching the average for a new car being $40,000. To me, that is flat out ridiculous. Not to mention financing has gone from a traditional 4-5 year car loan to 7-10 year for higher end vehicles. If you finance a vehicle for 10 years, you have made a terrible decision and purchased a vehicle you absolutely can't afford. You may be asking... *"What about leasing?"*

Absolutely not! Leases are the best possible deal for the car dealer and the worst for the consumer... don't do it!

HOW CAR LOANS REALLY WORK

Let's say you take out a car loan for $10,000 over 5 years at 5% interest. This is an interest rate based on good earnings and credit. Your total loan would be $10,500, spread over 60 months. That's $10,000 divided by 60, giving you a monthly payment of $175 a month. "Wait Gary! That is really easy..."

Not so fast. This example is actually incorrect. But the above example is how most people *think* this loan would work. In reality, car loans break down more like this...

Monthly payment: $188.71

Total loan payment after 60 months (5 years): $11,322.74

Total interest paid: $1,322.74

Here's what that would look like broken down by year...

Year	Interest	Principle	Balance
Year 1	$459.00	$1,805.55	$8,194.45
Year 2	$366.62	$1,897.93	$6,296.52
Year 3	$269.52	$1,999.03	$4,301.49
Year 4	$167.45	$2,097.10	$2,204.39
Year 5	$60.16	$2,204.39	$0.00

Are you confused yet? I am. And I consider myself to be pretty good at math. When it comes to the lending industry, nothing is simple—and for good reason. I actually read the formula on how a standard amortized car loan works and it absolutely hurts my head. One other thing you may notice is that, just like your good old mortgage, these types of loans are *front loaded* with interest. What does that mean?

It means that the two biggest loans that most of us use during our lifetime are completely rigged against us. Instead of the interest being spread out evenly over the length of the loan, which would be the fair way to do it in my opinion, interest is calculated daily. This means you will pay most of the interest on your loan during the first 30-40 percent of the life of that loan. Huh?

Yep, you got it! Every time we borrow money, we are getting completely screwed by today's banking system. Of course, the people who PROFIT from lending you this borrowed money will NEVER tell you this. Instead, they'll try to convince you that a car loan is another opportunity to "build your credit." They convince you of this for the same reason car dealerships and manufacturers try to persuade you that a more expensive car will make you either:

- Safe -- Which is how they typically target women.
- Smart, sexy, or sophisticated -- Which is how they typically target men).

So say you pay your 5-year car loan off after 2 years. Yay for you. Except the bank makes sure it still collects a majority of the interest on that loan. Don't get me wrong. Paying off that loan early is still a good thing. It's just not as good as you are lead to believe.

UNDERSTANDING THAT YOUR CAR IS A TOOL, NOT A STATUS SYMBOL

I know this is a hard one for people to understand today, but your car's primary purpose is to get you from point A to point B. Have you noticed those car ads always show people having the time of their lives and people staring at them in their new shiny car? The car manufactures and advertisers want you to feel like you are someone special and cool when in reality, you are purchasing a car for all the wrong reasons.

I look at my car as a tool in order for me to live the life I want. I spend over half the year in the mountains at my off the grid house and the remainder in my travel trailer. That's why I needed a heavy-duty truck, with four-wheel drive. And guess what? That's exactly what I bought. And it was the best decision I could have made as my vehicle fits my lifestyle perfectly.

What I *didn't* do was purchase the highest end version of my model truck. I bought the one that had all the options I needed, but nothing more. This cut tens of thousands off the price tag. That said, here is the number one and critical point... I could afford it and easily!

HOW I LEARNED THE HARD WAY WHEN IT CAME TO CARS

I purchased my first car when I was 15. I paid cash—a whopping $1,500 for a 1978 little Toyota pickup with 130,000 miles on it. It was all I had in my savings. But I had it, and it was what I could afford. I will say it was a great purchase for a first vehicle. It did everything I needed. It got me to school, sports practices, and my job (yes, I worked all through high school).

Once I left my small town, I got caught up in my "looking cool for the ladies" stage. Hey, I was teenager. What do you expect? I went on a binge of poor car purchasing decisions, squandering money I should have been saving. But I thought those cars were part of my image. But I was being something I wasn't.

After several reckless car purchases, I finally saw the light. Well, not completely. But I realized I could have a really good car for a great car price if I shopped around and bought used cars. I ended up buying three used sports cars over a 5 year period. Yes, I was still young and maybe just a bit immature. On average I paid 50% of the original sticker price, and made sure they were still under warranty. I was able to enjoy them for a while, and then sell them just before the warranty ran out. The best part - I broke even or made a little money on those three cars.

I learned two key lessons from this. First, pay cash, and get a deal on someone else's bad decision. The downside was it took a lot of work finding them, and I then had to sell them. But it did teach me that car loans suck, because I hadn't had one for 5 years, and realized used was the way to go.

Second, and probably the biggest lesson I learned was that by paying cash, I controlled what vehicle I could afford. Not some slick salesman or bank. Cars are known to be one of the biggest impulse buys we make. After all, no sales person can talk you into buying a car you can't afford if you have a limited amount of cash.

This is where most people go wrong. They "buy" the car with money they don't really have. Heck, you can now buy a car online. Just go pick it up off a glass carousel. No salesman needed. Now that might sound good. But I don't think it is. The easier they make it for you to purchase something you don't really need and cannot afford, the more your purchase benefits the bank or the sales person, instead of benefitting you.

HOW SMART CAR PURCHASES CAN MAKE YOU A MILLIONAIRE

To close this chapter, I'm going to do something a little different, as it is more than likely not the interest on a car loan that is going to get you. More than likely, it will be the act of purchasing an expensive impractical vehicle with long-term monthly payments.

For example, let's say instead of making the average $500 a month car payment for the next 40 years (again this is a static payment number it will go up, probably dramatically), you invest that $500 a month into an asset that earns you 5% interest per year over the next 40 years. Here's what that could do for you...

$500 per month, times 12 (months per year), times 40 (years), at a 5% compounding interest rate, equals $761,038.

In other words, that car that makes you look so cool or sophisticated will cost its driver about three-quarters of a million dollars. Think about that next time you see one of those "look at me and my cool car" commercials.

THE SOLUTION – A CAR THAT FITS YOUR LIFE AND SMART CAR SHOPPING

Below I will give you what I feel are the steps to getting the car you need, not the car you want. Yes, I know it's hard. I want a Ferrari, but a Ferrari won't help me live the life I really want.

1. If you cannot pay the remainder of your car loan off in the next two years, you need to sell the car and get one that fits your financial situation.
2. While it may not seem practical (or even be possible) right this moment, your next car purchase should be used and bought with cash.

3. Start saving now to purchase your next car, with cash.

4. Evaluate what kind of automobile you need in order to live your life, not to look cool. Come up with a list of practical and affordable vehicles that meet these requirements.

5. How long could you go without a car, while you save up money to buy a used one? Maybe you can eliminate owning a vehicle for a year or two in order to get your finances in better condition.

6. If you are a multi-car family, determine if you really need multiple vehicles, and eliminate the one that costs the most.

11

COLLEGE – A PH.D. IN FINANCIAL FANTASYLAND

To say today's education system is off the rails would be an understatement. What is taught in our schools today is a mix of consumerist indoctrination and twisted facts. Neither of which prepares you to be successful in life. Well, unless our definition of success is to be broke, sick, and unhappy. Think I sound fanatical? Take a look at the results our education system is producing. We're addressing many of them in this book.

If our education were actually preparing us to be the best we could be, the curriculum would be much different. Is it any wonder that most people lack the skills to balance their budget, live within their means, understand basic concepts of health, cook their own food, be more self-reliant and have the ability to simply look someone in the eye during a conversation?

These are the crucial skills we need in order to prosper. Yet, they are absent from the so-called "well-rounded" range of subjects being taught in our educational institutions. Throw in the fact that most college professors in public universities have little or no life experience in the subjects they teach, and the fact that they rarely, if ever, have their opinions challenged, and you have a perfect formula for a lifetime of Gridlock. The blind leading the blind, so to speak.

And guess what?! There are people who PROSPER as a result of you and I being sick, broke, and misinformed about how to succeed with our money. We've been talking about them in this book. You know those rules we talked about earlier? The ones that are designed to make you and I slaves of The Grid Game, while the people who MAKE those rules seem to win almost effortlessly, and at our expense?

Where do you think we learn most of those rules? How many times have you heard that the path to success and happiness is to graduate High School, go to a good college, build your credit, find a job, get married, "buy" a house, etc? Think about how much money moves out of your hands, and into someone else's as a result of HOW you carry out these decisions.

I don't say any of this lightly, nor to disparage education. I have three college degrees and have coached younger men and women in athletics and taught at the college level. Remember, "Knowledge is Power" was the first of the 5 Principles we talked about in this book. So I take education very seriously. I have said in the past "once you stop learning you are dead."

But it can be any plainer than this, in order for humans to be successful, happy and driven, we need a system which will help us learn from our more experienced elders. Without this system, humans would not last very long on this planet. But it's important to make the distinction between education, and indoctrination. And if what we're learning is making us broke and sick, while others are becoming richer and more prosperous, I'd say there's a whole lot of indoctrination being passed off as education.

THINGS HAVE CHANGED, JUST BECAUSE YOU ARE TOLD YOU NEED TO GO TO COLLEGE DOESN'T MEAN YOU SHOULD

If you're a part of my generation, or the one before me, you've heard this enough times to make you puke... *"If you want to be successful, you have to go to college."*

Sadly, it's no longer working that way for most college graduates. So where have we gone so wrong? College used to represent a place of higher learning. Now, I call it a place of higher *earning*; higher earnings for those who run the corrupt zoo that is still called "higher education." The instructors are supposed to prepare you for a successful profession. Proponents of higher education tell you that all the good careers require an advanced education.

And if you're not interested in pursuing such a profession, you can enter a trade usually as an apprentice and learn the skills from someone who was an expert in that trade. From there, you can stay in that trade by working for someone else or by starting your own business.

Both of these are important paths, and one is no better than the other. It used to be that a college education would give one a higher overall lifetime earning potential than those working in trade. In some instances, this may still be true. But those days are mostly gone. And yet, if you are motivated, you can make a very good living without a college education.

Meanwhile, a college education can put you tens of thousands, if not hundreds of thousands of dollars in debt, AND delay you for several years from getting started in your chosen profession. Those years matter. So do the subsequent years you spend paying off your college debt, with interest, while struggling to gain the needed experience and reputation in your field. And while you're playing catch up, the person who didn't go to college has already spent *your* college years gaining the entry level experience needed to move up into the job you MIGHT have been hired for if you'd spent those years getting the experience yourself.

And in case this is starting to sound like the rant of an uninformed fanatic, let me tell you a little about my educational background. As I have mentioned, I come from what would be defined as a poor family. Neither of my parents went to college. I believe both had GED's, neither completed traditional high school. So my motivation to attend college was to better my lot in life, and move up the "societal ladder."

This was not easy. There was no one paying my tuition or holding my hand. No one advised me of what to expect during my college experience. I arrived at college as a young man from a town of less than two thousand people, and was suddenly on a campus of thirty-eight thousand college students. To say I felt a bit overwhelmed would be putting it mildly. But, I persevered, working multiple jobs between classes, and made it. It took me a year longer than the normal 4 years to get my Bachelor's degree. But I made it.

But I didn't stop there. I went on for a Master's degree, while being enlisted in the Navy, and went on to get another degree while starting my entrepreneurial adventure. This was shortly after leaving the federal government, having worked in military intelligence and federal law enforcement for half my life. This also allowed me to teach at the college level, and that gave me a very different perspective on today's college education system.

Do I regret spending all that time in higher education? No. I learned a great deal of things outside of my education. It also became a part of who I am today—a teacher and educator of life simplification. But it is important to remember that this path is not for everyone. Nor is there anything wrong with you if you didn't, or couldn't, get a formal education yourself. This is one of the biggest problems in our college education system – the story that says everyone who wants to be successful should go to college.

That is just flat out bullshit. And it's perpetuated by an inflated bureaucracy that rakes in huge amounts of money, off the backs of hard-working people like you and I. College is not for everyone. But if we tell people that it is, we end up cranking out college graduates like widgets, until there's no place to put them in the workforce.

Not to mention that the increased demand allows colleges to pad their degree programs with worthless nonsense. For example, what's the point in getting into heaps of debt for a degree in bi-sexual, gender neutral, religious studies of the 15th century? Is it going to better your lot in life? Enough to make up for the debt? Ok, I made that one up for dramatic effect. But I've lost count of the people I have met who have completely useless degrees in subjects I have never even heard of. But, here is the catch…

When I first enrolled in college, 30 plus years ago, getting one of these marginal degrees wasn't as devastating as it is today. It didn't have the tragic financial impact on your life that it does now. For one, college was far cheaper, and fewer people were attending than today, thus making the value of a college degree much higher. It was also easier to find ANY job, by having ANY degree, because college graduates were still rare.

Fast-forward to today, and college is irrationally expensive. Financing a simple Liberal Arts degree, with very little earning potential, can run you six-figures and THAT can drastically derail your ability for financial success and freedom.

To put this into perspective, let's break out some basic 5th Grade level math…

30 years ago, when I was earning my first degree, it cost around $1,200 a year for tuition and books. This was to attend a State college in California. Between working, and getting some scholarships, this was easily obtainable for me, or any hard-working young person. I did take some student loans my last

year of college, but at a $4,500 total, these were still pretty manageable. But here is the key...

I could have attended a much more expensive private college. But I did this nutty thing called math and realized I couldn't afford it. Not to mention it made no sense for me to go that route even if I could. And as you might have guessed, I wasn't too egotistical to attend a State College. I didn't let the needling of my peers or of society convince me that people who attend State Colleges are somehow less sophisticated or that their education is inferior as a result. How many people heap tons of soul-crushing debt onto their shoulders because they THINK they have to go to an expensive college to impress their peers, or even their prospective employers?

College isn't about where you go to school. It's about how you apply yourself. Ask someone who actually hires or manages people and I bet 90 percent of them will tell you the same thing. This is why, when it came time for me to decide where to go to college, and how much money to spend, I applied simple math, and some common sense, and made a decision I could live with.

Now, let's contrast that with the average cost of college today...

According to U.S. News, the average tuition for in-state public college for 2018-2019 was $9,716 a year, compared with $35,676 for a private college. They also mentioned that more than 100 private colleges were charging $50,000 or more in 2019.

This shows an 8 fold (that's 800%) increase compared to what I paid to attend an in-state college, just 30 years ago. I find it strange that all these "equality for all" pundits say college is "the big financial equalizer," when the cost for college is expanding at such an outrageous rate! So the way to shrink the financial inequality gap is to pay a drastically over inflated price for college, and to finance it with money you don't have? I smell a rat!

And by the time you graduate college today, it's totally possible for you to owe what a home would cost in some parts of the country. If you and I can't see the absurdity in this, we need a nice smack in the face to be woken up.

According to today's "rational" of "college for everyone" (which last time I checked, anyone can attend college if they want to) taking on massive debt, right out the gate of your life, is supposed to help you gain financial prosperity in the future. Meanwhile, people who don't go to college are busy gaining real-world experience and advancing in the jobs YOU'LL be competing against them for, as you step out of college with no experience at all.

Sure, this might work out for a select few. But good old 5th Grade math tells us that college education is not the fairy tale we've been sold.

And if that's not bad enough...

THE COLLEGE LOAN CRISIS IS A BUBBLE WAITING TO BURST

As I write this, the Federal Government is lending out money for college as if they money grew on trees. Because of this, demand is increasing and colleges are raising tuition at a rate that would make wartime oil price hikes look pretty. This is a prime recipe for a financial bubble, and we all know how hard those bubbles can hit the entire nation when they pop. And let's add some alarming statistics about student loan debt:

- Federal student loans are the only consumer debt segment with continuous cumulative growth since the Great Recession.
- Student loans have seen almost 157 percent in cumulative growth over the last 11 years.

- As of 2018, we have more than $1.5 trillion in student loans. According to the Federal Reserve, this makes it the second-largest consumer debt segment in the country, just after home mortgages.
- Outstanding student loans make up more than $500 billion of total credit card debt in the United States.
- Student loan debt currently has the highest 90-day plus delinquency rate when compared to all other types of household debt.
- Among the Class of 2018, 69% of college students took out student loans, and graduated with an average debt of $29,800.
- 44.7 million Americans have student loan debt.
- The average monthly student loan payment (not in deferment) is $393.

Now, let's crunch the above numbers so we can add it to our ever-growing, lifetime "pissing away my money" equation. Just for simplicity, I'm going to use the average $393 student loan payment (per the 2018 data above). Student loans are pretty standard with 10-year payment terms. So our math will look like this:

$393 times 12 (months a year), times 10 (total years), equals $47,160.

Note: This is just borrowed money. It doesn't include what you paid out of pocket for college.

Are you starting to see how the system gets you little by little? Are you starting to realize how those little bits add up to big losses over time?

Let's take another example. This time, let's combine the

three main expenses you will more than likely have at this early stage of your life:

1. Your car loan: $500 a month.
2. Your Student loan payment: $393 a month.
3. Your credit card payment: $358 a month.

Total monthly debt: $1,251

So, if you were to follow the commonly accepted path to prosperity, you would have an estimated $1,251 of monthly debt to pay off right out of college. And that's when you're barely out of your teenage years. Now, let's talk about the "payoff."

As of 2018, the new college graduate makes an average of $50,390 a year.

Now take your $1,251 per month in debt payments, multiply it by 12 (months per year), and you've got $15,012 in total debt payments per year.

If we subtract your estimated yearly salary of $50,390, you're left with $35,378 per year.

I know what you're thinking: "After I get out of college, even with that average debt load, I'm still better off than most. And once I pay of the debt, I'll be flush with cash."

Here's why this is just another logical train-wreck of an assumption...

First, we haven't factored income/state taxes in yet. You also have to pay health insurance, car insurance, oh, and that minor matter of eating and having a place to live. So let's add these into the mix and see where you are now...

- Taxes - $16,780 per/yr
- Car insurance - $2,400 per/yr
- Medical insurance - $6,000 per/yr

- Rent and utilities - $12,000 per/yr
- Food - $6,000 per/yr

Keep in mind that this is purely dependent on what state you live in. But I think a safe number to go with paying federal, state, and remaining payroll taxes (FICA) is going to be about 33%, which is purely from my tax-paying experience over the years. So, your total expenses are $43,180 per year.

Oh, and let's not forget to add your $15,012 in debt payments…

Uh-oh Houston we have a problem! According to these numbers you are going to be short at least $7,802 a year. Guess what most college graduates do when they discover this? They use their credit cards to make up for that $7,802 yearly short-fall. And thus, they go on digging themselves into deeper debt.

Here is a big one…

Have you noticed that the above has no deductions for retirement or 401k contributions? And the above has also left out going on vacations, or attending events you might enjoy. So you are not only broke, there will also be no fun time to go along with it! I guess I just threw another couple of spoonfuls on that shit sandwich.

Now I know these numbers are open for debate. But I always try to use the most conservative numbers I can. The important question is, what can you do about this?

INTRODUCING GARY'S RULES AND RECOMMENDATIONS FOR COLLEGE

This chapter was not meant to discourage anyone from attending college. Actually this may surprise most, but I think you should definitely go to college if you want to pursue a career, which requires a college degree. But let's be clear that I'm talking about careers like:

- Medical/Nurse/Doctor/Psychologist/Psychiatrist
- Engineer
- Law
- Scientist
- Software/Computer Science (not always)
- Teacher
- College professor

This is not a complete list. But if you want to pursue a career, or shall I say "life purpose" (I cover an entire chapter on life purpose in my book The Simple Life Guide To Decluttering Your Life), you need to think long and hard whether college is the best way to go. If your career isn't on the list above, college might not be the most *practical* path for you.

Here is a critical point I want to drive home...

Going to college doesn't guarantee success. It doesn't give you any special advantage over others. For me, as a business owner who sometimes hires people, it primarily means that you dedicated yourself to a series of steps in order to earn a piece of paper. Other than that, it is 100 percent about how you make yourself an asset to me and my company. I don't care about your GPA, special activities, or class rank. In order to succeed and be an asset to your community and this planet, you are going to have to work hard and prove yourself. And that's true whether you have ten degrees, or zero degrees. And when it comes to that, trust me, no one gives two shits what college you went to.

I will say this with absolute certainty: I have met more millionaires without college degrees than I have met millionaires WITH college degrees. Think about that. Again, this is not to discourage you. But college is a tool in life, not a golden ticket. In the book *Emotional Intelligence* – the author Daniel Goleman found that 15% of success could be attributed to training and education, while 85% was attributed to attitude, perseverance, diligence, and vision. And no, those weren't "made up on the spot" statistics like some of these self-help authors tout. This is an author who did his homework. Read the book. You'll see.

Now I will contradict myself a bit, and say that if you have no clue what you want to do in life, college may be a good idea. Case in point, I was an idiot from age 18 to 25. Some may say I still am, but I think I have progressed a bit. But this is true for most young adults. They don't know what they want to do with their lives, and often change their minds frequently.

So, instead of spinning your wheels and playing "musical jobs" just to pay the bills, attending a junior college might not be a bad idea. Plenty of people find their passion in life while sitting in a college classroom. The key is to do it WITHOUT accumulating debt. Financing your way into trying to figure things out is a terrible idea. Bottom line, if done correctly, college can't hurt. But doing it because everyone else is doing it or because you can finance the entire four years of keg stands, that's going to keep you on the treadmill of bad financial decisions possibly for decades after you've graduated.

So, the take away from this chapter is that everyone doesn't need to go to college to be successful. But if you do decide to go that route, do the research. Make sure you can afford it. Find out how much it will cost you, how long will it take, and whether your career choice offers enough financial reward for it to make sense. And for God's sake, don't study something just because someone else thinks it's a good idea or because you think you can make a lot of money. No amount of money is worth being stuck in a career you're not passionate about.

Can you save money (best option pay cash) to go to a cheaper smaller college, or start at a junior college before transferring to a 4-year institution? I've met many people who dug a huge hole, filled with debt, to get a teaching or counseling degree. It took them years and years to pay off those loans, putting them AT LEAST a decade behind on their goal of achieving financial freedom.

And finally, for those parents who want to help their kids with college (I don't mean paying people to take their SAT's, or bribing University officials with truckloads of money) by putting together a college savings plan I'm all for it. But that doesn't mean that just because you saved for their college that you should force them to go.

Also, I advise not to give them any free rides. Pay for part of it, but not all. I can tell you this first hand, I had a far better work ethic, and an actual resume for my first job, because I was gainfully employed all through college. Meanwhile, my cohorts who had their parents pay for everything did not work, and didn't develop this work ethic because of it. All they learned was how to sleep in, watch Gilligan's Island re-runs, and get straight C's. Hard to justify paying for their entire education, when it keeps them from developing the basic skills to apply to the real world. Remember Principle #2: Avoid Extremes. Your child needs to find their own rhythm in life, and your part in that is to avoid the extreme of giving them too much.

By now, we've talked about the high cost of poor health decisions (eating out) and the lifetime cost of other early life financial decisions. Now, let's have a look at the one life decision will can make or break you financially...

12

THE BUSINESS OF MARRIAGE – WHAT'S LOVE GOT TO DO WITH IT?

L et me start off by getting everyone's underwear all bunched up!

I do not personally believe in the *legal* institution of marriage. Hear me out before you throw this book into the fire. I do believe in relationships and love between two individuals or for that matter whatever floats your boat. As long as it doesn't cause harm to others. What I don't believe in is government agencies being involved. By that, I mean the bureaucratizing of our personal relationships. As you might have already guessed, what I'm saying is that the legal institution of marriage can be an obstacle to financial freedom. It has become a place for The Gridmasters in government and big business to skim more money from us.

I believe, what I like to call "institutionalized marriage" has become part of the false narrative about how to find happiness. Our indoctrination into Poorville starts with our initiation into the serf-making school system. After that, we have the debt ridden trip to college, followed by an unfulfilling job in a cubicle, then institutional marriage, followed by home "ownership", and finally, having kids. Every one of these steps has the potential to lead us deeper and deeper into financial bondage. And your final reward, to die shortly afterwards.

Sure, sign me up! I'm all in.

There are massive industries that revolve around you getting married (and divorced --more on that later) and spending a butt load of money doing it. I mean, what better way to start off your life together, then by living with false societal expectations and being tens of thousands of dollars in debt!

So let's take a look at the numbers and see just how much today's wedding industrial complex is costing us.

40K FOR ONE DAY, WE JUST KEEP SPENDING LIKE IT JUST DOESN'T MATTER

According to a 2016 Real Weddings Study from "The Knot" (this was a survey of nearly 13,000 actual brides and grooms across America) the average cost of a wedding is $35,329. That doesn't include the honeymoon. For that, we'll throw in another $4,466. So the average married couple is looking at spending $40,000 for one day… makes total sense, right?

Keep in mind that the above numbers are only an average. My research showed that if you get married in Manhattan, NY your wedding and honeymoon would cost closer to $100,000!

For me, this is nuts. The average couple is spending more money in one day than I paid to get my three college degrees, and to purchase my first three cars… wow! Heck, that is close to half of what I paid for my first house!

But, of course, these youngsters are flush with cash, right? Yes, that was sarcasm again. And since the couple is normally broke, guess where the money for that expensive wedding comes from? Yep, more than likely it comes from glorious credit cards. I know what you're thinking… *"But Gary our parents are paying for our wedding!"*

How does that make sense when the couple COULD have a modest ceremony and use the money their parents would have spent on the wedding to help them buy a house instead? Nevertheless the data tells us that the couple's parents likely don't have a pot to piss in themselves. So they are more than likely financing your fairy tale day on credit cards or a home equity line of credit. This is the insanity of a young couple blowing $35,000, or more, on ONE DAY of their life.

Yet, ironically, most people think that they can solve their financial problems by "making more money." Is it starting to become clear, that we have a spending problem, not an earning problem? Six figures for a wedding and honeymoon is some serious cash, but it appears a lot of couples are doing just that. Especially considering these are usually young people who are still paying car payments, student loans and either renting, or paying a mortgage.

Add to this the fact that the couple is likely decades from reaching their full earning potential, and we're talking about a big, big chunk of money. The data tells us that before you are out of your twenties, you'll have accumulated enough debt that it could take decades to pay off. The plan has worked perfectly, for the banks. For you, not so much. You are now financially trapped, and will be a slave to debt for the remainder of your life. All as the result of bad decisions which were completely avoidable. And, even if you manage to get partially out of debt prison...

DIVORCE, MORE PEOPLE WAITING TO PICK AT YOUR CARCASS

At this point, it shouldn't surprise you that, just like marriage, divorce is a huge business in this country.

If you are saying, "We love each other and are happily married so this doesn't apply to us," keep in mind that...

1. Every couple says that at some point in their marriage.
2. Even if you think you'll never divorce, the statistics say otherwise.

It was a little tricky to get solid numbers, but from what I found, it appears that 50 percent of first marriages, close to 70 percent of second marriages and about 75 percent of third marriages end in divorce. Is it any surprise to you now, why divorce is such a big business? Imagine running a business where your product or service could be marketed to half, or more, of all married couples? And from the couple's perspective, just think about this. When you shovel out those five or six figures to legally "tie the knot," you have *at least* a 50 percent chance of losing HALF of your stuff, and accumulating several thousand dollars (or more) in legal fees, just to untie that knot another ten years later.

Would you take your life savings, and even borrow more money to gamble it on these types of odds? If you said yes, we are going to have to get you in a math class, and quickly!

I'm not sharing all this doom and gloom to discourage you from pursuing marriage or building a family. But I want you to have the real information, so you can make an educated and *non-emotional* decision about how to go about it. Because here is the kicker, guess what the number one reason is for divorce?

If you guessed money problems, you're right. And who couldn't have seen that one coming?

So, what we have is young couples, trying to get their start in life, piling on mountains of debt to get married, than taking on more debt to buy their "family home," and other "necessities," to create the same financial problems that end up destroying their marriage, and sending them into a second financial tornado when they get divorced. Remember Principle #2: Avoid Extremes, and honestly ask yourself how you could possibly call this anything but extreme.

So how much does the average divorce cost? The numbers were a bit all over the place, but most of my research indicated it is in the $15,000 - $20,000 range. I'll be honest, I have known many people who have been divorced over the years and only a couple came in under the above number. When you figure the average divorce attorney charges $250 an hour, is it any wonder why the average divorce takes years to finalize? There is no benefit for the legal system or the attorney's to have your divorce quickly and easily resolved. I have seen it time and time again. The divorce lawyers pitting the couple against each other, draining every last dime they have. And guess what happens when the money runs out? The divorce finally goes through. My, what a coincidence!

Are you starting to see how pursuing the "American Dream" is making everyone rich, except you? Just think about what the average kid or teenager looks forward to: getting an education, finding a good career, owning a home, getting married and having kids. All of these things make them a "money target" for businesses.

And these numbers are just the beginning when we consider that some people will get married and divorced more than once during their lifetime. Again, I'm not trying to discourage you from getting educated and starting a family with someone you love. But it's worth asking how much of that is YOUR dream, and how much is just a fairy tale put into your mind by aggressive marketing campaigns.

YOU ARE NOT A PRINCESS AND MARRIAGE IS NOT A FAIRYTALE

The biggest piece of hogwash rational I hear, when it comes to blowing ridiculous amounts of money for a wedding is "this is my special day." Yes, I will agree that it is. But what does wasting a bunch of money you don't have, have anything to with making the day "special?" Is it really worth it when that one day makes most of the following years financially harder? I like to call this the "fairytale effect." It's another tool to keep you locked in The Grid for life. Women, and in some instances men, have been brainwashed into thinking their wedding day is supposed to represent some kind of fantasy. And of course, this fantasy is the product of marketing campaigns pushed by the same industries who will profit from expensive weddings.

I know some of you might be rolling your eyes saying, "Here goes the life-long single guy giving me love and marriage advice." Yes, it is true I have been single all my life, but I have participated in many weddings. Also, keep in mind that this is financial advice, not relationship advice. Although, the idea that blowing a bunch of money on an expensive wedding will make your *marriage* a fairy tale is a horrible way to think about relationships too. People caught up in this delusion aren't in a place to make sound decisions about money, or marriage. So, in my opinion, my place as an unemotional observer makes me much more objective than the bride or the groom.

Think of it this way, if you were told marriage was a special day for just you and your family, to be held in a private setting, away from all the hoopla, who could profit from that? Yep, no one. Instead, it would be a day to honor your love for each other, and that has nothing do with money.

You have to get out of this "I'm a princess" and "this is my day, I want the perfect wedding" mindset. That is just what they want you to think. You have to start thinking about your life together AFTER the ceremony that life won't be perfect because relationships never are. So why sink yourselves into debt, right out of the gate, trying to create the "perfect day" to start it all off?

MAKE IT ABOUT LOVE AND STARTING OFF WITH LESS STRESS AND OUTSIDE EXPECTATIONS

Wouldn't it make more sense to take that $40,000, the amount the average couple spends on a wedding, and put it to work on a future of living debt free and happy? Instead of obsessing over the $2,000 you're going to spend on the perfect table settings, and the other $38,000 worth of decorations and other crap, let's brainstorm some smarter and more positive ways to spend that money. For example, you could...

1. Use the money to pay off outstanding debt. You know, those student loans, credit cards, and car payments we discussed earlier.
2. Use it to pay for your first house with cash (more on that later).
3. Use it to purchase a dependable, low maintenance vehicle.
4. Invest it.
5. Use it to start your own business.

For me, it just makes sense to live in reality, and to realize that spending a ton of cash on your wedding day is not going to make you love each other more. It won't make your marriage last longer (statistically speaking it's more likely to make it shorter). I've probably been too close to fifty weddings in my life, and the most enjoyable for all have been the ones done on the cheap in someone's backyard. No freak out moments about things not being perfect. No stressing over pictures that cost several thousand dollars. No $250 a piece table settings that go right in the trash five hours later. Imagine that. Just a bunch of friends and family enjoying your dedication to each other.

On a final note, I would argue that today's societal expectations that you "must get married and have children as soon as possible" has actually *created* our high divorce rate. I know I have felt the pressure over my life to get married and have a family. I believe many people today are rushing into relationships and getting married before they are ready. How many times have you heard someone say that they got married because they were "sick of dating and wanted to have kids?" How many single people are sick of their family pressuring them to have kids or get married?

How many people say "we're already living together, so we might as well be responsible and get married?"

In my opinion, those are pretty bad reasons to make a life-long commitment to another person and to starting a family. Especially considering the financial consequences we just talked about. Sure, Thanksgiving dinner might be less enjoyable when you hold off on getting married and have to listen to the needling of your family members. But you have to think about what's best for you. Not to mention, divorces have a tremendous negative impact on the children who are caught in the crossfire. Think about them, and your future, and make the smart decision. Not the decision everyone else THINKS you should make.

Now that we've stamped out the standard fairy tales about how to be happy, let's use our heads. Let's talk about how to spend your money on things that will make your life better. This means those slimy divorce lawyers and $250 an hour Wedding Planners might have to do something productive instead of sucking off your misery. My guess is you won't lose any sleep over that though.

13

YOUR HOME – THE AMERICAN DREAM OR FINANCIAL NIGHTMARE?

I f there is one thing in this country that our society uses to measure "success" or "making it," it is home ownership. I pursued this "dream" and purchased (mortgaged) my first home when I was 28 years old. I remember thinking "wow I have achieved the American dream!" I used my VA loan, basically putting as little a down payment as possible, and paying Private Mortgage Insurance (PMI). In case you're unaware, PMI is arranged by your lender and provided by *private* insurance companies.

PMI is usually required when you have a conventional loan and make a down payment of less than 20 percent of the home's purchase price. PMI usually goes away once you've paid off 20 percent of your home's value. But before this happens, you throw away hundreds of dollars a month by having PMI. The lesson I learned from this first home purchase is that if you don't have at least a 20 percent down payment, you shouldn't be purchasing a home. More on this later.

I have owned a total of 1 condo, 2 four-plex apartment buildings, 1 preexisting home (a real estate flip), 3 new construction homes, and 10 land lots (I still own 9 of these lots).

In addition, I had my real estate license for 8 years, and real estate was my first side business venture as an entrepreneur. So, I have a good deal of experience when it comes to real estate, and it took me years to learn some very hard lessons about the financial facts of home ownership.

WHAT HOME OWNERSHIP REALLY COST – A LITTLE SECRET THE GRIDKEEPERS DON'T WANT YOU TO KNOW

Today home ownership is in nutty land, as far as I'm concerned. Home prices have skyrocketed yet again, especially in those hot zones, such as Los Angeles, Washington D.C., New York, and the Silicon Valley. The prices today in many areas have eclipsed, in some cases greatly eclipsed, the housing boom bubble of 2008. This means we still haven't learned our lesson. Let's take a look at the average price of a pre-owned and new construction homes today.

- According to the latest information (March 2019), the U.S. Census Bureau reports that the average cost of a new construction home is $376,000.
- According to the latest information (March 2019) by the National Association of Realtors, the average sale of a preexisting home is $259,400.

Here are the top 5 most expensive housing markets in the United States as of 2018:

1. San Jose-Sunnyvale-Santa Clara, California $1,250,000
2. San Francisco-Oakland-Hayward, California, $952,400
3. Urban Honolulu, $812,900
4. Anaheim-Santa Ana-Irvine, California, $799,000
5. San Diego-Carlsbad, $626,000

And, the 5 *least* expensive housing markets in the United States, as of 2018:

1. Decatur, Illinois, $89,300
2. Youngstown-Warren-Boardman, Ohio, $97,200
3. Cumberland, Maryland, $109,100
4. Elmira, New York, $111,400
5. Erie, Pennsylvania, $113,300

Listed below is what you need to earn in a year in order to live in the most expensive cities in the U.S.

1. San Jose, CA: $274,623
2. San Francisco, CA: $213,727
3. San Diego, CA: $130,986
4. Los Angeles, CA: $114,908
5. Boston, MA: $109,411
6. Seattle, WA: $109,275
7. New York City, NY: $103,235
8. Washington, DC: $96,144
9. Denver, CO: $93,263
10. Portland, OR: $85,369

There are no misplaced decimal points or commas – in San Jose you need to make over a quarter of a million dollars in order to live today. I don't show you all this information to discourage you. I want you to understand that homeownership in this country today is serious business. As with many Americans during the last housing bubble, I had to make some critical financial decisions regarding my future.

Of all the purchases in your life, your home will by far be the most critical and expensive one you make. Again, no one teaches this in school. Don't you find it strange that the most critical financial decisions most of us will make in life aren't even discussed in our education system? Huh, I wonder why. I have a pretty good idea though.

If people knew how home loans truly worked, and the costs associated, I bet a great deal more people would put off home ownership, or at least put more thought into the process. But if we did that, the banks couldn't give their CEO's and board members multi-million dollar bonuses and stock options. Oh, and when they screw up, guess who has to bail them out? That is right…you and me… the hardworking taxpayers. Remember at the beginning of this book when I differentiated between greed and a legitimate desire for money? There is no better example of this in our financial institutions than the people who run them.

I want to give you the low-down on what homeownership will really cost you. Neither your mortgage company or real estate agent will ever share this with you. Now, there are many factors that will determine how much you will pay in interest, insurance, PMI, etc., over the life of your loan. But I want to give you a very basic tabulation. If you take out the standard 30-year loan, near or around current interest rates (2019), you can expect to pay double the price of your home. This means that if your home costs $250,000, you will pay in the neighborhood of $500,000 by the time you've paid off your loan. Of course these aren't exact numbers. But I have found the doubling of the original purchase price of your home to be a fairly accurate calculation for the total cost of a loan.

So, if you follow the traditional 30-year loan, which almost everyone does, your home will cost you close to a half-million dollars by the time you've paid it off. Oh, and it gets better.

During those 30 years, you will more than likely do a couple remodels, repairs, landscaping, and see increases in property taxes, insurance and just general maintenance costs. This can easily add another $250,000 to the total cost of your home. Meaning, your home could end up costing you three-quarters of a million dollars, or more. And that's just to own the average American home, according to 2019 prices. Boy oh boy are we broke yet?

Again, you are seeing how all the pieces of the "debt for life" puzzle come together? I have already shown some pretty devastating numbers when it comes to your finances. That is, if you follow the path you've been told to follow.

The primary fact though is that most Americans never finish a 30-year loan because they either buy a bigger more expensive house as their earnings go up, or they move to another house and reset their 30-year mortgage. Most of us never consider how this actually exasperates an already massive problem by sucking up our potential for financial freedom. Let me show below how this works.

According to the best data I could find, it appears Americans stay in their home around 6 to 7 years. Again, this is not perfect. But from my own personal experience as a homeowner, this sounds fairly accurate. Using these numbers, the average American will own around 10 different homes during their lifetime. Again, I like round numbers, so 10 works pretty well, and at this time I'm on pace to own around 10 homes. That is, if I live to, or around, the average lifespan of American men today.

What does this mean in the big picture? It means that it is possible with the above numbers we could have up to 10 home loans during our life. Remember me discussing at the beginning of this book how home loans are front loaded with interest? Let's use the average numbers and assume that you'll spend about six years in your house before moving to a new one.

I'll use that pesky math again to prove my point.

In the below example I will be using the average cost of a pre-existing loan in 2019 dollars ($259,400), financed with a 30-year loan at 5 percent interest rate, assuming you've put 20 percent down (i.e., $51,880). I'm being pretty generous with the above numbers, just to try and equal out the discrepancies of poor data. After all, most Americans will not qualify for an interest rate of 5 percent, and almost no "homeowners" have $50,000 to use as a down payment.

If you sell your house after 6 years, your principal and interest numbers will look like this:

- Interest paid after 6 years: $59,322.72
- Principal paid after 6 years: $20,885.28

Do you now see how the interest is front-loaded? Your total interest paid on the entirety of this loan would be $193,530.10. So, by you paying $59,322.72 in first 6 years, you are paying 30.65% of the interest, even though 6 years only represents 20% of the life of the loan. Think about that for a moment, and consider how many people believe that renting is a waste of money. And when you consider that most people move before they've even paid off ten years of their mortgage, it becomes obvious that most "home ownership" payments go towards putting money into the Bank's pocket in the form of interest.

I know what you are thinking because I thought the same thing before I crunched the numbers years ago, "but Gary I have paid down $20,885.28 in principal so at least I will get that back when I sell the house!"

Not really, and here is why – you will have to pay the real estate agent fees of 6 percent. Yes this can be negotiated sometimes, but let's use the standard rate just to be realistic.

We will also use the standard level of appreciation used in the real estate world of 3 percent a year. Sometimes I come out ahead. Sometimes I don't. Appreciation is very subjective. But I like to use the lower number instead of a high number, just to be on the safe side.

So 3 percent compounded yearly over 6 years using $259,400 (average cost of American house 2019), equals $309,737.17

Now we must determine how much we will pay in real estate agent fees:

6 percent times $309,737.17 equals $18,584.23

Now, we subtract $18,584.23 from $309,737.17, giving us a total of $291,152.94

I will warn you that this is going to get a little complicated, and guess what? That is exactly how "they" want it to work. The more complicated the math, the less attention the average home buyer will invest into understanding this, and the easier it will be for the Gridkeepers to profit from that complexity. The average person will never run the numbers and determine the actual cost of a house "bought" on a 30-year mortgage. Matter of fact, I would guess the average real estate agent lacks the basic skills to even do this tabulation. But remember Principle #1: Knowledge is Power. The goal of this Chapter is to equip you with the knowledge about who actually benefits from home "ownership."

To get our true rate of return after the sale, we have to determine ALL the costs that go into mortgaging the house. This means we must subtract the principal paid to date from original price ($259,400). This is the balance of what you owe at time of sale. Then, we subtract that from $291,152.94, which is your sale price after real estate agent fees. Again I'm being generous, as I haven't included loan origination fees and hosts of closing costs, which vary greatly depending on where you buy your house.

I will also not factor in 20 percent down payment, as that

represents money you already had, so it doesn't count as profit. I will elaborate on this detail later.

So the above initial equation will give us $259,400 (Original sales price), minus $20,885.28 (principal paid to date), yielding $238,514.72.

We can now subtract what you hypothetically owe from estimated profit, minus real estate agent fees, which would look like this…

$291,152.94 minus $238,514.72 equals $52,638.22

This is your total estimated profit after sale so far. But we're not done yet.

So our profit after owning our home for 6 years is $52,538.22. Woohoo! That's enough to buy your new mid-life crisis Porsche!

Not so fast grasshopper! We have some more math to do. And I will warn you it is not in your favor. You must factor in all the interest you paid on your handy dandy *front loaded* mortgage.

$52,538.22 (profit after sale), minus $59,322.72 (interest paid to date), gives you a negative $6,684.50!

Uh-oh! Houston we have a problem! What happened to your profit? It vanished in a puff of financial institution smoke! Ok, so if we look at you've lost, $6,684.50, and consider that you've lived in the house for 6 years, that is not so bad. After all, you need a place to live, right? Yes you do. But we forgot something the pesky cost of owning a house…

There are a lot of things people don't see, which cost a good chunk of money while owning a home. As a homeowner for most of the last 20 years of my life, I consider the list below a pretty accurate example of these hidden **monthly** costs of owning a home:

- Homeowner association fees (HOA) $300
- Homeowners Insurance $100
- Taxes $200
- Utilities (electric, water, trash) $300
- Yard upkeep $100
- Improvements/repairs (again I'm being very generous) $150

Total hidden monthly costs, $1,150

Now we need to figure out the 6-year cost by adding these hidden expenses:

72 (months), times $1,150 (additional home costs), plus $6,684.50 (taken from above tabulated loss during sale), equals $89,484.50 in additional ownership costs over that same six years.

This means our total cost of home ownership over that six years, after it is sold, is **$89,484.50.**

After owning a home for 6 years you are almost $100,000 in the hole! Well, that does not look like what all the investment gurus, real estate geniuses, and banking institutions told me. How about you?

But now, a little good news…again you have to live somewhere, so now let's figure out your cost of living per month while owning your dream home…

$89,484.50, divided by 72 months, equals $1,242.84 per month.

So your total cost per month while owning your home is $1,242.84.

Using our above 20 percent down, and 5 percent interest rate, your monthly payment would be around $1,500—not including taxes and insurance. Factor those in and you are probably looking at closer to a $1,700 or more for your monthly payment. The fact that most people never calculate these numbers doesn't change the fact that they add up without us realizing it.

Just as an example - let's say that instead of using $51,880 of free cash for a down payment and purchasing the above average house, I paid $300 a month to rent a space to live in my RV. This is what I paid while building my off the grid house. I could potentially save $1,400 a month for (12 months), and 12 times $1,400 would equal $16,800 a year in savings. If I were to save more money on top of that by living debt free, and my income kept increasing, it is not unrealistic that I could purchase my next house with cash in another 5 to 10 years. This would mean NO a mortgage at all while still having a place to live.

You might choose to save up 40 to 50 percent instead of taking this route. But I just throw this out there to show you that there are many options to outsmart the system. Again, I hear it already "I can't do that Gary!" Look if you start any sentence with "I can't," which most Americans do when confronted with change, I will pretty much guarantee you will not accomplish *anything* you set out to do. Remember Principles #4 and #5: "Something is Better Than Nothing," and "Take Action Today and Every Day." If doing all of this at once sounds overwhelming, you can always do something, and repeat that every day until you find your rhythm and start developing habits and seeing real changes.

The above final numbers on house ownership are a far different number than what we have been lead to believe. Everyone tells you that home "ownership" is the road to your dreams and to riches. Huh, I guess I wasn't paying attention in math, because my numbers say something different. Of course, every real estate market is different. But keep in mind that these numbers also assume that everything goes pretty much the way you expect it to, with no unexpected expenses and that rarely happens in life. Throw in a possible real estate crash and the numbers can be flat out devastating.

The primary way you are tricked into thinking that you came out ahead is in your closing statement. I'm talking about when you sell your house for a "profit." It only shows the profit from what you owe (amount financed minus principle paid to date) and the sales price minus real estate agent fees and other closing costs. Your down payment, interest paid, and those darn forgotten about monthly cost of ownership costs are never tabulated. Thus the numbers are greatly skewed in the end, making you look like a winner when in actuality you are a loser in the financial game. In order for you to turn an actual profit (gaining more than you spend while owning your home) your house value would have to almost double in price during those 6 years.

I will not even get into how the system is rigged against you on the commercial real estate side (apartments are considered commercial real estate). There is a formula that the commercial real estate agents use to price a property basically insuring you will never make a dime owning apartment complexes if you finance them with a 20 percent or less down payment. The people who make money on commercial real estate either time the market just right, or they pay cash and get good deals on the properties they purchase. In other words, the main people who make money on small apartment complexes are the real estate agents and banks. I know this one first hand, as a former small apartment owner. Oh how cash is king, and those who have most of it make the rules!

This is by no means to say that owning a home or investing in real estate is a mistake. I love my home, and I have made some good money in the real estate market. But it is a definite liability when you follow what the system leads you to believe is the road to prosperity. My main goal in this chapter is to show you the true numbers of home ownership. Not the BS, some dimwit financial advisor or real estate agent barfs into your lap. I have broken out these numbers to a couple of supposed personal financial experts, and they left with their mouths wide open in disbelief. Guess where I first heard "well you need to live somewhere?" Yep. You guessed it. From financial advisors and real estate agents.

But the numbers don't lie. Are you starting to see why, if you do not understand basic math, the system will drain you dry? The people who run this system know that you will never take a look behind the numbers curtain, you'll keep falling into their web. It's no wonder why we're broke. They're teaching us exactly what they want us to learn, and we're paying for it.

THE SMART WAY TO HOME OWNERSHIP THAT THEY NEVER TOLD YOU ABOUT

Now that I have dashed your hopes of ever owning a home, let's take a look at a solution that's grounded in sound math and common sense.

This is how you make savvy financial decisions in the real estate market, and make money instead of handing it to greed-slick bankers and realtors...

1. Never finance a home without at least a 20 percent down payment, and with no more than a 15-year mortgage. The 20 percent down will save you from the dreaded PMI sinkhole, and will get you a better interest rate in most

cases. If the loan officer tells you a 15-year loan is not a smart move and will cost you more, smack them in the face… just kidding. But you get the point. Using the example outlined before, the same house, financed over 15 years, will save you in the neighborhood of $150,000 over the life of the loan. That's compared to then 30-year counterpart of that *same* loan. Yes, your monthly payments will be more. But more of that money will be going into building equity in your home. That's a much better way to go long term. Ok, I just read your mind. You are saying "I'll take out a 30-year mortgage and pay it off in 15 years. That way I have some breathing room if I need it!" The majority of Americans today have proven that they lack financial discipline to do this. And, like you and me both, they usually tell themselves that they're the exception to this rule. So get that "that won't happen to me…" thought out of your head! Simply put, if you have a 15-year mortgage, the worst-case scenario it is that you'll pay it off in 15 years. Not to mention that if you plan to pay it off in 15 years anyway, why take a longer mortgage in the first place?

2. Never use your home like a credit card. In other words, don't get a home equity loan or a line of credit, then use it to buy that really cool boat. If you do this, the truth is that you can't afford the boat. Taking out the loan is a direct denial of that fact.

3. Don't think it is a smart move financially to buy a home as a tax right off. First, that deduction is not safe, as we have recently learned. Second, exchanging a couple thousand dollar tax right off for hundreds of thousands of dollars in debt is about as stupid as it gets.

4. Don't say "I know I will probably ("probably" is a curse word when it comes to personal finances) live in this house less than 6 years, so I'll get an Adjustable Rate

Mortgage (ARM)." ARM's are adjusted according to prevailing market interest rates. So if things go south during that six years, you're screwed! You could even end up stuck in the house for much longer than six years because you can't sell it. Do you remember that financial crisis 10 years ago? Guess who were the big losers? Those who had ARM loans. Why add risk to the biggest investment you will make in your life if you don't have to?

5. Don't buy the BS that owning and financing a home is a great investment. That is one of the biggest lines of bullshit we have been sold. A home is a place to live. When done correctly, it can be a smart investment. But we just proved that when you look at the numbers, you will more than likely lose money by "owning" (mortgaging) a home with the traditional 30-year loan.

OWNING YOUR HOME OUTRIGHT THE REAL WAY TO FINANCIAL FREEDOM

I know most of you are saying that owning your home outright and not having a mortgage is dreamland fairytale. But I will tell you this with 100 percent certainty, the people I have met who paid off or paid cash for their homes are the *most financially free people* I have met. I have not had a mortgage payment for 10 years now. I own my off the grid home, with 40 acres, free and clear, and it is fantastic. It took me 40 years to learn this lesson. But better late than never.

You may be saying "So, what if I already have a mortgage?" There are many options. But the best is to pay it off as soon as possible. This will probably involve some pain. But again, that is what it takes. The key is that if you follow what I have outlined prior, and later, in this book, you will have plenty of extra money to achieve this.

.   .   .

There are two primary ways I recommend that you do this:

The first - is to refinance your 30-year loan into a 15-year loan.

The second - is to make additional payments towards *your principal* (which, again, is the amount owed on your loan, minus interest). Do this every single month. For example, let's say you owe $200,000 on the average American priced house of $259,400, with a 30-year loan. If you were to pay an additional $1,000 towards your principal (which after you cut out all the fat of your finances, should be easily doable), you would pay off your loan 19 years, 8 months early and save $130,201.80 in interest.

I know when it comes to paying off your house early, people will resist this tooth and nail. They'll do this because they've been programmed to believe that having a home loan is "just a fact of life." Maybe it is for people who want to stay on the treadmill of financial slavery. But for those who want true freedom, this is a must.

If you haven't purchased your first house, you are in prime shape to do things right and to avoid the pain and the wasted money, just as I have. Simply put, you need to save, save, and save. Again, if you follow all the methods and avoid the typical financial pitfalls I have outlined, you can pay cash for your first house. The most important thing to remember is to buy what you can afford to *buy*, not what some dimwit real estate agent or financial institution tells you to buy. I would highly recommend you purchase a fixer-upper and learn those crazy things called life skills. Most people today have no idea how to fix a leaky faucet, and will pay someone $100 or more an hour to replace a washer or tighten a nut.

When I bought my first house, I remodeled the entire place myself. I didn't have a clue what I was doing. I started by reading a ton of remodeling books. But even with that, there was a lot of trial and error. I continued to build on those skills, and they have saved me hundreds of thousands of dollars over my lifetime. There is no doubt in my mind that without learning the above decades ago, I wouldn't be in the great financial shape I'm in today. In addition, by learning these basic skills, I now have a higher quality home, built the way I want it.

The benefit of purchasing a fixer-upper and doing the work yourself will be additional equity. This will give you a nice little profit when you decide to sell your home. All you need to do is repeat this for each house, and in a short period of time, you will have your dream home, debt free. Trust me, I kick myself all the time for not doing all this when I was younger.

Finally, if you really want to go on an adventure, you could explore the mobile lifestyle in a RV, until you save enough money for your first home. This was the route I took during the building of my off the grid home. Matter fact, I still live in my RV part of the year.

14

ARE YOU A SLAVE TO FASHION? YOU ARE BROKE, BUT YOU LOOK COOL!

I'm just going to say it… fashion is utterly stupid! The fact our lives revolve around something that, in almost all cases, has nothing to do with being happy, and is designed ONLY impress other people, is pure insanity. Especially considering that most people are too busy obsessing about how they look to even care about how anyone else looks.

Our current desire to mass consume clothing, accessories, to spackle our faces and acquire all the other "bling" associated with it, shows once again that we have lost our collective minds. The concept of fashion and beauty originally derived from the upper crust of history. The primary goal was for snotty elites to impress or "outdo" their counterparts. In most cases they did this out of sheer boredom. When you have ridiculous amounts of money and free time, why not play dress-up and have parties, while the masses are dying of smallpox and starving? Makes total sense right?

But as people moved up the social ladder, someone figured out a new way to fleece the average person. They could create a market that remains in continuous change, requiring you to buy more and more just to stay "in fashion." And if you don't buy the latest fashion garments, you are not cool. I remember when dressing for summer meant putting on shorts, and winter meant putting on pants and a coat. Not today, if you want to be considered part of todays "buy everything in sight" society, your fashion must constantly change. Oh I know, some of you are already saying "Of course, a redneck like Gary would say something 'like fashion is stupid.'"

Yep, as I sit here writing my next book in my non-trendy workout clothes, in which I actually performed exercise in earlier, you are 100 percent right. But after you read this chapter, I think you'll see how much money you are wasting trying to be cool or to fit in. I think you'll agree that staying fashionably relevant has nothing to do with how the world really works.

I guarantee by the end of this section you will be shocked by the numbers. I know I was. Of all the things making you broke, including your car, house, college debt, etc., fashion is one of the biggest whammies for most of us-- and by a large margin. Bet you didn't see that coming, did you?

Let me share how our trendy sense of "fashion" it is making us broke in the process.

- According to the most recent Consumer Index by the Bureau of Labor Statistics, the average American household spends over $1,800 a year on clothing and services.
- The U.S. apparel industry today is a $12 billion business.
- In 1930, the average American woman owned nine outfits. Today, the average figure is 30 outfits – that's one for every day of the month!
- The average American throws away 65 pounds of clothing per year.

- Americans spend more on shoes, jewelry, and watches ($100 billion) than they do on higher education.
- A Consumer Reports National Research Center poll of 1,057, (prepared for the shopping magazine "ShopSmart"), found U.S. women, on average, own 19 pairs of shoes, although they only wear four pairs regularly. It also revealed that 15 percent of women own over 30 pairs.
- Shopping malls outnumber high schools.
- 93% of teenage girls rank shopping as their favorite "pastime."
- Women will spend more than eight years of their lives shopping.
- A survey of 3,000 women, aged 16-75 years old, found the average American woman will spend up to $300,000 on face products alone in her lifetime. She'll also throwaway, having never even used, nearly two-thirds of these products. Men don't get off the hook either. According to another survey, it is estimated that men will spend close to $175,000 over their lifetime on products to improve their appearance.
- One in twelve women admit to reapplying their lipstick up to nine times per day. And researchers found that most Britons refresh their deodorant or perfume three times a day, while one in four (25 percent) check the mirror six times or more a day.
- A new report from the American Society of Plastic Surgeons (ASPS) reveals that Americans spent more than ever before $16 billion on cosmetic plastic surgery and minimally-invasive procedures in 2016.

The above numbers and facts are staggering to me, and I hope they are to you as well. Matter of fact, this may surprise most, but it appears we will waste more money on fashion and beauty products than we do on the average American home with a 30-year mortgage. Just wait until I break down the numbers below. You will be able to buy a couple homes, with cash, using the money you blow trying to look cool!

Ok, women not to pick on you, but one of the above really stuck out to me – "women will spend more than 8 years of their lives shopping." If we use 18 years old (an adult) and the average lifespan of a woman which is 81 years today. That gives us a total 63 years for women as an adult. I know this is not an exact science here, but bear with me on this. According to these numbers, you will spend 13 percent of your life on this planet shopping. Just think, if we subtracted out 16 more hours to factor in sleep and possible work hours… oh heck why not let's do it.

Our math will look like this:

(63 years as an adult), times (365 days in year), times (24 hours in a day), equals 551,880 hours of total life expectancy.

To make it more realistic, let's subtract out work hours (job related), from weekends (26 weeks in year), times (2 days for weekend), that's 52 days.

(52 days in year for weekends), times (63 years of life as an adult), times (8 hours to account for hours not worked during weekend), equals 26,208 hours.

To give us a more realistic number, we will add 26,208 back in below. Just to account for the hours which don't represent possible shopping hours. Now I'm being generous, as most people will go shopping during lunch or online during working hours. But hey I'm feeling nice at the moment!

Now we need to factor in 8 hours a day for sleeping (63 years as an adult), times (365 days in year), times (8 hours a day for sleep), and we have 183,960 for possible total sleeping hours.

Now we'll add another 183,960 for your work hours.

So now 183,960 plus 183,960 equals 367,920 total hours of life you have available for non-work, non-sleeping activities.

551,880 minus 367,920 equals 183,960 plus 26,208 to account for weekends not working. That's 210,168 total possible hours that you're not either working or asleep.

I know your eyes are probably crossed at this point, but just a couple more steps.

To get your lifetime shopping hours, we go (8 years), times (365 days in a year), times (24 hours in a day), equals 70,080. That's more than 70 thousand estimated hours of your adult life you'll spend shopping.

So now, your total time spent shopping, during the hours while you're not either working or sleeping, is about **33.3 percent!** How many OTHER activities do you think you spend a third of your recreational hours doing?

We have lost our friggin minds, and our wallet's it appears! Today's women will spend one-third of her waking non-working hours shopping!

If it is not crystal clear from above why you need a firm grasp of basic math in order to be financially free, I honestly don't know what else to do to prove my point. For most people, the time and money wasted on meaningless things and/or activities never becomes "real" because they never quantify it as I have in this book.

But wait! That is just a taste of financial poo pie for this section. We haven't even dove into all the spending numbers yet.

Before we do that, I want to explain something, as some of you are probably going "what an old fart! He probably walks around in his knee high tan socks, with his goofy polyester pants or shorts, velcro shoes, and big collar polyester shirt! What does he know about fashion?"

Wait a second…is what I just described cool right now? Maybe just the big collared shirt, the shoes… oh wait, they used to be cool. Now they're not. So, what should I buy now?

Honestly, I have to say that I don't understand the point of chasing ever-changing trends. What if certain foods were in style, or out of style? Would you be worried about whether you looked "cool" while you were eating? What was uncool last year is now cool this year and visa versa. It never ends. On top of this, you're supposed to dress "right" for the season. I'm sorry, I just don't have the time for such things. I have better things to do with my life, and my money. Which makes you wonder whether people chasing these trends have anything better to look forward to.

One of my favorite recent trends is the hipster movement. It is dumbfounding to me that a guy would grow his hair out purposely so he can put it into a bun (the famous manbun) and wear a thousand dollar outfit with accessories to look like a skinny logger! Not to mention that he looks down on "those Neanderthal loggers…" see the ridiculous irony? Stupid, stupid and more stupid. How about those skinny or bedazzled jeans (jeans with big pockets with stitched bling-bling) for guys… you have to be kidding me. If you are a guy, and have been a part of these trends, spending money and time while constantly complaining about not having enough of either, please slap yourself, or just whip your unbridled manbun in your face. And don't worry about your man card. That fell out of your extra-large bedazzled pocket a long time ago!

Ok, that was a tangent. But I felt it was important to break out some numbers to show how much time we waste on this, just to reinforce my point. But on top of the wasted dollars and cents we can't ignore the lost time and energy that goes along with it.

Now let's get into the meat of this section.

Let's add up the amount of money we spend looking, in most cases, foolish. All for the sake of pursuing the ultimate me, me, me society.

These are the really tough facts. We will use the lifetime spend on beauty products of $300,000 for women and $175,000 for men. Again I think these numbers are very safe, as more than one woman told me my numbers were low, possibly over 25 percent too low.

For clothes, I will have to estimate using the following math:

(The average family spends $1,800 per year on clothes), divided by (Average family size – 2018 – of 4 people), times (79 years – average lifespan), equals $35,550 *per person* estimated lifetime total spent on clothes.

Oh, but wait. I didn't forget one - in our narcissistic society today we have one more number… plastic surgery!

According to the latest numbers from the U.S. Census Bureau, there are 251,918,924 adults (18 or older). So using the average numbers, our math will be:

($16 billion dollars in cosmetic surgery procedures), divided by (251,918,924 adults in U.S.), times (78.7 life expectancy in years), equals and average of $4,997.45 per person spent on cosmetic procedures during their lifetime.

Now the itemized tally:

- Amount women spend on beauty products during their lifetime: $300,000
- Amount men spend on beauty products during their lifetime: $175,000
- Amount the average person spends on clothes during their lifetime: $35,550
- Average lifetime amount per person spent on cosmetic surgery: $4,997.45

Total for women: $ 340,547.45
Total for men: $ 215,547.45
Total for a married couple: $556,094.90

A married couple could buy two plus average American priced homes with cash if they just forwent the boob jobs, skinny jeans, makeup, and smelling like a toxic flower from Mars. What are your thoughts on the "hip today gone tomorrow" fashion and beauty product world now?

I'll be honest. I had no idea the numbers where this big before I started doing my research. And when you factor in the time spent shopping for these items, including time spent in plastic surgery and recovery time, I believe this could possibly be the second biggest elephant in the room, just after health. Oh and by the way that tummy tuck and boob job aren't going to make up for those thousand calorie lattes and fast food stops.

HOW TO PROPERLY DRESS ON A BUDGET AND MAYBE EVEN LOOK COOL AT TIMES

I have used a system to save money on clothes for decades now. As a result, I spend a very small fraction of what the average American will spend in a year. I don't roll around in my leopard skin pants and turquoise tank top from the 80's as some might think. Again, I look at my apparel as a tool of my lifestyle. Not much has changed. Here are a few helpful tips. These may be different for women, but probably not as much as some might think.

1. Always purchase your clothes on sale. I have a couple favorite companies mainly for outdoor gear, and I know what time of the year they have their blowout specials up to 50 percent off. A simple way to find sales – purchase winter gear at the end of winter, purchase summer clothes at the end of summer.

2. Never buy clothes just because you are bored, or shopping for the sake of shopping. For example, I never go looking for clothes unless I'm looking for something specific that **I NEED**.

3. Be consistent with your style. People who criticize you because you dress sensibly, and not for the latest fad, are losers… ignore them.

4. If you have to dress up or somewhat dressed up for work limit yourself to 5 outfits, and mix them up. Trust me, most people can't even remember what they ate for breakfast, let alone what you wore yesterday or the day before. If you don't wear a suite, don't buy one unless/until you need it.

5. Get your clothes from a second hand store in an uppity part of town. There is some gold in those mines for pennies on the dollar.

6. Rotate your clothes – my workout clothes are also my

mountain and road biking wear, then my pajamas, then outside work clothes, finally to the rag bin. I will easily get 7-10 total useful years out of one set or workout clothes.

7. If it is trendy, ignore it. In 6 months, you will be uncool for wearing it just as quickly as you were cool for wearing it.

8. If you are buying clothes to draw attention to yourself, you need to get your priorities in order. I'm not saying looking good for special events is a no go, or that it should be frowned upon. But the moment you start thinking "look at me," for the sheer sake of it, you've forgotten what is important in life.

9. This is one I just don't understand… spending stupid amounts of money on infant and small children's clothes. They have no idea what they are wearing and don't care. It is all about the parent saying "look how cool my kid looks." I think kids should run around like little banshees, not giving a rats ass how they look. Get your young kids clothes from other parents who are giving them away, from thrift stores or even from your older kids hand-me-downs. If you want to throw money in the fire, buy trendy clothes for your small children. Not to mention all the time you waste finding those darling little outfits.

BEAUTY IS NOT SKIN DEEP

Now, let's talk about beauty products. I know this sounds cheesy, but your beauty does come from the inside, not the outside. A good-looking asshole is still an asshole! Instead of focusing on the superficial you, work on living a simple happy life and being a better person. If you spend all your time worrying about what others think and how you look, you're in for a long and unsatisfying life. Not to mention we all get old and wrinkly at some point… then what?

Can you guess what the most popular cosmetic surgery is today? According to the American Society of Plastic Surgeons (ASPS)? Breast augmentation. Oh boy. Where to start on this one. As a guy, let me tell you there is nothing that is more of a turn off than a pound of makeup on your face, and/or fake breasts. For someone who primary cares about the character of individuals and their actions in life, this says it all to me. If you are focused on one person and one person only (yourself and how you look), you are not ready for a meaningful relationship anyway.

You may say I just don't understand because I'm a man. Yes and no. If you are doing that to attract a partner, I really don't think fake boobs and a makeup caked on your face is the best way to go. We already know the divorce rate is basically a coin flip in this country. Why would you want to spike those odds for yourself by attracting a mate using your superficial attributes? For me, it makes no sense at all. But I like to live in reality, where big fake breast, or those calf implants for the guys, don't make your life any better. They will cost you a lot of money, and a good deal of pain or even possible death. After all it is a complicated surgical procedure.

Now for you primped up, supposed men, pull your head out of your ass! What are you doing spending $175,000 over your life time on men's beauty products? Just think of all the time and money you have wasted, and for what? You are not a fashion model. You're not on the cover of GQ. And the woman you're looking for isn't going to care whether you were or not. Take that money and spend it on something other than spritzer for your hair, or some foul cologne that I could use to run my backup generator.

People may misconstrue what I have just said as me saying it's okay to be a slob or not care about your personal appearance. I get that. You can't just show up to work in your pajamas or workout clothes. Heck, I specifically remember a guy I worked with who we had to tell to go home and take a shower. Don't be that guy.

But be sensible about it. Your clothes are not who you are. They are something you wear in order to accomplish a task, nothing more. I hear the excuse all the time, "my clothes make me feel good about myself." That would be like me saying "my hiking boots give me confidence to be the best I can be." No, they help me go climbing, hunting, and hiking! If I needed them to do more than that, it would be time to change my attitude, not my clothes.

The slogan "Image is everything" has made us into a bunch of self-centered wimps, lost in our world of make-believe. We need to live in reality, and focus on getting our shit together, especially financially. We are the most prosperous country in the world, and all we do is complain about how unfair it is and how we don't have enough money. Trust me, I know the system is a nasty one run by a bunch of shallow greedy individuals who look at us as pawns in their game. But you know what? We can still control our ability to earn, spend and live the life we want. It is about taking responsibility for our actions. Instead of saying "I can't" we need to learn to say "I need to fix this, how do I do it?" not "I can fix this if I just buy another $60 shirt."

The right mindset is the key to financial freedom. I should know. I had to figure it out myself as well. The freedom and life I live now wouldn't be possible without me saying enough, and doing something about. I can guarantee one thing... you will not change anything by complaining and trying to cover it up with a tummy tuck, skinny jeans (you need the tummy tuck first for these) or stinky perfume.

When you take your last breath, no one is going to care whether you had nice tight skin on your face or that you were a trendy dresser. Try to imagine someone saying that at a eulogy, "Dave was an asshole, but man could he dress!" Anyone who cares about these things probably doesn't have a clue what type of person you were while you were alive anyway, and is at your funeral for the food and to hit on the single women, and probably the married ones as well.

If it's a choice between being fashionable and being financially free, a smart person will choose the later. Let everyone else go broke trying to impress other broke people. There are more important things in life, and we'll talk about them in the next Chapter.

15

PUTTING ALL THE PIECES TOGETHER - YOU ARE A POSSIBLE MULTI-MILLIONAIRE AND DON'T EVEN KNOW IT

When I first started this book I knew the numbers were pretty bad. But I didn't expect just how bad they would be. Throughout my life, I have worked hard to avoid and correct the financial pitfalls along with the traps set up by our mass consumer system. I had tabulated numbers here and there. But writing this book made me dig deep and crunch numbers like I had never done before. In many cases, the results left me speechless. We don't just waste money, we spend ourselves into oblivion-- and on the most useless and stupid crap known to man.

Now it is time to put all the above pieces together and paint the entire picture. As I have said many times, this is not an exact science, as I had to make some assumptions. But I tried to be as conservative as I could be. Now, we will go section by section to arrive at a possible total of the money we will waste during our lifetime. I'm using the average numbers per person, as it would get complicated to figure it out for families--having too many variables.

I will say this, these calculations are the biggest elephants in the room. There are a whole host of other things we blindly blow money on. Many, which we can't afford at all. Things like vacations, boats, motorcycles, junk food, jewelry... I think you get the point. I also understand not everyone will go to college, get married, purchase a home etc. I computed these numbers with the average American in mind, as an attempt to show how much money we really waste on "stuff."

This is just for example purposes, so please... no nasty emails about how I don't know what I'm talking about. I firmly believe the numbers I have come up with could easily be doubled if we factored in every bit of frivolous spending. Also, remember many of these were based on 40-year work estimates, so again I was very conservative. And finally, these are today's numbers. So they are static estimates. They will most definitely be much higher as you factor in future price increases and inflation.

We'll start by recapping the totals according to their Chapter...

1. Chapter 7 eating out $193,440
2. Chapter 8 not saving while young $12,000
3. Chapter 9 credit card interest $49,437.60
4. Chapter 10 car payments $240,000
5. Chapter 11 college loans just one degree $47,160
6. Chapter 12 wedding (assuming you have just one) $35,329
7. Chapter 13 interest home loans 10 moving every 6 years over lifetime $593,227.20
8. Chapter 14 fashion and beauty $340,547.45 (women) $215,547.45 (men)

*I will use two different totals for men and women due to the large difference in lifelong spending on fashion and beauty.

TOTALS:

Men: $1,386,141.25
Women: $1,511,141.25

Yes, those are two commas. So we're talking about more than a million dollars per sex. For married couples, you can add up the two numbers to get your total of nearly $3 million! I think it is pretty crazy using very, very conservative numbers I was able to come up with close to $1.5 million in wasted money per person. Now I realize some of these expenses cannot be avoided. But at the very least they could be drastically reduced.

How about some real fun now? More math! Let's assume you invest this money instead of spending it on useless crap. What would you have at the end? I think the 40-year career in the workforce is a good timeline to work with. We will base this on a consistent monthly investment (hence the static number), and based on the above totals.

(40-year work career), times (12 months in a year) = 480 months total.

For men ($1,386,141.25 estimated wasted earnings during lifetime), divided by (480 total months during earnings career), equals $2,887.79.

That's the total amount a man could invest monthly if he started spending responsibly.

Again, we will use the very conservative number of 5 percent as our investment return interest rate. Most investment books use 10 percent as the rate of return on investments, so I'm using half that number. So, if you invested $2,887.79 every month, at 5 percent yearly return on investment you would have $4,281,226.74.

I'll give you a second to get over the shock.

For women ($1,511,141.25 estimated wasted earnings during lifetime), divided by (480 total months during earnings career), equals $3,148.21.

That's the total amount the average woman could invest monthly.

Again, I will use the very conservative number of 5 percent as our investment return interest rate. If you invested $3,148.21 every month, at 5 percent return on investment, you would have $4,667,305.80.

Yep, that is right! Not only would you be a millionaire, you would be a multi-millionaire! What do you think of all that useless junk you waste money on now? Does it make you happier than having several million dollars in the bank?

Let's have one last bit of fun. Let's see what your monthly interest income would be with the above amounts, again using 5 percent.

After factoring in inflation and taxes, you could expect to bring in around $20,000 or more a month without touching your initial investment balance.

Do you think can you live off $20,000 a month during retirement? Are you starting to see how this consumer and debt based economy is absolutely crushing your ability to live a financially secure and a free life? I think I have proven that we all have the capability to be millionaires. We just have to be smart with our money. We ignore that we are the richest people on the planet and just demand more and more. Even though it is pretty obvious, to me, that we just spend ALL of our money, no matter how much we have. As I said before, it's not as much about how much you make. It's about how smart you spend/invest it.

MY FINAL THOUGHTS

I have noticed that in our society, instead of figuring out what is truly important in our lives, and how to build a better future, we just make excuses. We say, "If I had more time…" while we spend an average of 7 hours a day watching TV, on the internet and yelling at people we don't know on social media. We say "if only I had, more money…" while we spend every dime we have and more, having less than $1,000 in savings. We say "My job doesn't pay enough…" or "We need a higher minimum wage…" while it appears that no matter how high the minimum wage goes, we will just blow it and ask for more. Trust me, I have been in the same mindset… "I just need more money and every-thing will be fine," instead of living within my financial parame-ters and being debt free.

I will tell you that we live in the most financially stable and free society on the planet. Don't get me wrong. We have a lot of problems in this country. And you will not hear me argue against the greedy politicians and the rich getting richer at our expense. But the flip side of that coin is that every single person has the opportunity to be financially free in this country.

As I mentioned earlier in this book, the poorest people in this country are some of the richest people, when compared to the rest of the world. We are simply addicted to self-destructive spending habits. Again, I will not argue we have been programmed to be this way. There are a lot of companies and individuals who are filthy rich because of this, and they just want to be richer. What will equal the playing field (and trust me, they do not want an even playing field), is for us to be financially responsible and to live debt free.

If we as individuals were to do this, you would see all these hyper-consumption-based industries go out of business, overnight. Heck, those politicians and other Gridkeepers might actually have to go get a real job. Oh, we can only wish, right?

Income inequality is a very complicated issue. But only when people lack the proper information in order to fix the problem. The entire goal of this book was to show you that financial freedom is within your grasp… no matter who you are. You just have to be willing to focus on the things that matter and not get caught in the vortex of what "they" want you to do. My goal was to inspire you to focus on what you should do for *yourself, your family* and your community.

I truly hope you will find your purpose and passion in life, I hope this book helps you do that. That's all I can ask. I don't do this for fame and money. Just to put a pinch of my ingredients into the positive-change pie.

For those of you who would like to share your story of positive change, I would love to hear about it. I still answer all my emails, which is getting harder all the time. But is easier than most, because my followers are out there making it happen instead of emailing me pictures of their cat!

If you're subscribed to my newsletter, you can just respond to any new update email, or sign up for my newsletter at:
https://www.thesimplelifenow.com/newsletter

Finally, I want to thank all of you for making this possible. Without you reading my books, and the continued loyalty of my followers, I wouldn't be able to pursue my life purpose--which I consider myself very lucky to be able to do.

Now get out there and make it happen!

A LITTLE HELP FROM MY FRIENDS

Did You Enjoy This Book? You Can Make a Big Difference and Spread the Word!

Reviews are the most powerful tool I have to bring attention to "The Simple Life" brand. I'm an independently published author. That means, I do a lot of this work myself, from the writing, to the production, design, publishing, marketing, customer service, etc. This helps me make sure the information I provide is straight from the heart and based on my experiences. Rather than allowing some publishing company to dictate my agenda and delivery.

This means you, dear readers, are my muscle and marketing machine. Not only that, I truly love my fans and the passion they have for my writing and products. Simply put, your reviews help bring more fans to my books and attention to what I'm trying to teach.

So, if you enjoyed this book, please help me keep this operation independent of the big book publishers. You can do this by spending a couple of minutes to leave a review. It doesn't have to be long, just something conveying your thoughts. You can do this by going to www.amazon.com and leaving a review on this book's page, or my author page.

Thank you!

Gary Collins

ABOUT GARY

Gary Collins has a very interesting and unique background that includes military intelligence, Special Agent for the U.S. State Department Diplomatic Security Service, U.S. Department of Health and Human Services, and U.S. Food and Drug Administration. Gary's background and expert knowledge bring a much-needed perspective to today's areas of simple living, health, nutrition, entrepreneurship, self-help and being more self-reliant. He holds an AS degree in Exercise Science, BS in Criminal Justice, and MS in Forensic Science.

Gary was raised in the High Desert at the basin of the Sierra Nevada mountain range in a rural part of California. He now lives off-the-grid part of the year in a remote area of NE Washington State, and spends the rest of the year exploring in his travel trailer with his trusty black lab Barney.

Gary considers himself lucky to have grown up in a small town from a very young age where he enjoyed fishing, hunting, and anything outdoors. He has been involved in organized sports, nutrition, and fitness for almost four decades. He is also an active follower and teacher of what he calls "life simplification." Gary often says:

"Today we're bombarded by too much stress, not enough time for personal fulfillment, and failing to take care of our health... there has to be a better way!"

In addition to being a best-selling author, he has taught at the University College level, consulted and trained college level athletes, and been interviewed for his expertise on various subjects by CBS Sports, Coast to Coast AM, The RT Network, and FOX News to name a few.

His website www.thesimplelifenow.com, and *The Simple Life* book series (his total lifestyle reboot), blows the lid off of conventional life and wellness expectations, and is considered essential for every person seeking a simpler, and happier life.

OTHER BOOKS BY GARY COLLINS

The Simple Life Guide To Decluttering Your Life: The How-To Book of Doing More With Less and Focusing on the Things That Matter

The Simple Life Guide To RV Living: The Road to Freedom and the Mobile Lifestyle Revolution

The Simple Life Guide To Optimal Health: How to Get Healthy and Feel Better Than Ever

Living Off The Grid: What To Expect While Living the Life of Ultimate Freedom and Tranquility

Going Off The Grid: The How-To Book of Simple Living and Happiness

The Beginner's Guide To Living Off The Grid: The DIY Workbook for Living the Life You Want

REFERENCES

For a full list of references go to:

https://www.thesimplelifenow.com/financialreferences

NOTES

NOTES